Modern Critical Interpretations

T. S. Eliot's
The Waste Land

Modern Critical Interpretations

These and other titles in preparation

Modern Critical Interpretations

T. S. Eliot's
The Waste Land

Edited and with an introduction by

Harold Bloom
Sterling Professor of the Humanities
Yale University

Chelsea House Publishers
NEW YORK ◇ PHILADELPHIA

Library of Congress Cataloging-in-Publication Data
T.S.Eliot : The waste land.
   (Modern critical interpretations)
   Bibliography: p.
   Includes index.
   1. Eliot, T. S. (Thomas Stearns), 1888–1965. Waste land.   I. Bloom,
Harold.   II. Series.
PS3509.L43W3815   1986   821'.912   86-6064
ISBN 0-55546-0380-0

Contents

Editor's Note

This volume gathers together the best criticism devoted to T. S. Eliot's *The Waste Land* during the last quarter century, arranged in the chronological order of its original publication. I am grateful to Christina Büchmann for her assistance in editing this book.

The introduction centers upon the poem's covert relation to the work of Walt Whitman, and to "When Lilacs Last in the Dooryard Bloom'd" in particular. Hugh Kenner, ideologically the most Eliotic of all Eliot's critics, begins the chronological sequence with a reading of *The Waste Land* that essentially allegorizes or ironizes it as a High Modernist, neo-Christian critique of "the death of Europe." In direct contrast, Graham Hough views the poem as one of the very mixed aesthetic consequences of Imagism, and so as severely lacking in rational order, unlike the characteristic work of W. B. Yeats.

Richard Ellmann, analyzing the poem's manuscript versions, concludes that Ezra Pound as the poem's revisionary guide was able to do for Eliot what Eliot could not do for himself. In a comparison of *The Waste Land* with the descents to Hades in the *Odyssey* and the *Iliad*, Bernard F. Dick shows how profoundly Virgilian the poem is, in some of its aspects.

In a remarkably subtle essay, Eleanor Cook maps *The Waste Land* so as to expose its juxtaposition of London and Rome, and its deliberate failure to blend those cities of the mind into Jerusalem, the center of Dante's cosmos. Grover Smith, the most thorough student of Eliot's sources and structures, follows with another mapping operation, relating the poem's intended structure to its "mythical method."

A very different sense of Eliot's relation to literary tradition is manifested in the two remaining essays, by Gregory S. Jay and Cleo McNelly Kearns, a sense in which the editor's introduction shares.

Jay, working partly in the deconstructive mode of Derrida and Lacan, reads *The Waste Land* as an achieved anxiety of a Whitmanian kind, a "recurring dread that his poetic springs have run dry." Finally, in a brilliant exegesis that concludes and rounds off this volume, and is published here for the first time, Cleo Kearns gives a definitive account of the poem's relation both to Bertrand Russell and to Walt Whitman (an odd couple indeed!), and subsequently illuminates the literary persona that is voiced in *The Waste Land*.

Introduction

Eliot's *Ara Vos Prec* (London: The Ovid Press, 1920) contained a curious, rather flat poem, oddly titled "Ode," which he sensibly never reprinted. It appears to lament or commemorate his failed sexual relationship with his first wife, and strangely connects the failure with two Whitmanian allusions ("Misunderstood/ The accents of the now retired/ Profession of the calamus" and "Io Hymen, Hymenae/ Succuba eviscerate"). Manifestly, "Ode" mocks Whitman's erotic declarations, but the mockery is equivocal. Eliot's declared precursors form a celebrated company: Virgil, Dante, the English Metaphysicals and Jacobean dramatists, Pascal, Baudelaire, the French Symbolists, and Ezra Pound. His actual poetry derives from Tennyson and Whitman, with Whitman as the larger, indeed the dominant influence. Indeed, Shelley and Browning are more embedded in Eliot's verse than are Donne and Webster. English and American Romantic tradition is certainly not the tradition that Eliot chose, but the poetic family romance, like its human analogue, is not exactly an arena where the will dominates.

The Waste Land is an American self-elegy masking as a mythological romance, a Romantic crisis poem pretending to be an exercise in Christian irony. Mask and pretence, like the invention of more congenial fathers and ancestors, are customary poetic tropes, and certainly not to be censured. They are part of any poet's magic, or personal superstition, and they help to get authentic poems written. *The Waste Land*, rather than *Four Quartets* or the verse dramas, is Eliot's major achievement, a grand gathering of great fragments, and indisputably the most influential poem written in English in our century. I read it, on evidence internal and external, as being essen-

1

tially a revision of Whitman's final great achievement, "When Lilacs Last in the Dooryard Bloom'd," ostensibly an elegy for Lincoln, but more truly the poet's lament for his own poethood. Elegy rather than brief epic or quest-romance, *The Waste Land* thus enters the domain of mourning and melancholia, rather than that of civilization and its discontents.

Many of the links between Eliot's and Whitman's elegies for the poetic self have been noted by a series of exegetes starting with S. Musgrove, and continuing with John Hollander and myself, and younger critics, including Gregory S. Jay and Cleo McNelly Kearns, whose definitive observations conclude the book I am now introducing. Rather than repeat Cleo Kearns, I intend to speculate here upon the place of *The Waste Land* in Romantic tradition, particularly in regard to its inescapable precursor, Whitman.

II

In his essay, "The *Pensées* of Pascal" (1931), Eliot remarked upon Pascal's adversarial relation to his true precursor, Montaigne:

> One cannot destroy Pascal, certainly; but of all authors Montaigne is one of the least destructible. You could as well dissipate a fog by flinging hand-grenades into it. For Montaigne is a fog, a gas, a fluid, insidious element. He does not reason, he insinuates, charms, and influences.

Walt Whitman, too, is "a fluid, insidious element," a poet who "insinuates, charms, and influences." And he is the darkest of poets, despite his brazen self-advertisements, and his passionate hopes for his nation. *Song of Myself,* for all its joyous epiphanies, chants also of the waste places:

> Of the turbid pool that lies in the autumn forest,
> Of the moon that descends the steeps of the
> soughing twilight,
> Toss, sparkles of day and dusk—toss on the
> black stems that decay in the muck,
> Toss to the moaning gibberish of the dry limbs.

No deep reader of Whitman could forget the vision of total self-rejection that is the short poem, "A Hand-Mirror":

Hold it up sternly—see this it sends back, (who is
    it? is it you?)
Outside fair costume, within ashes and filth,
No more a flashing eye, no more a sonorous voice
    or springy step,
Now some slave's eye, voice, hands, step,
A drunkard's breath, unwholesome eater's face,
    venerealee's flesh,
Lungs rotting away piecemeal, stomach sour and
    cankerous,
Joints rheumatic, bowels clogged with abomination,
Blood circulating dark and poisonous streams,
Words babble, hearing and touch callous,
No brain, no heart left, no magnetism of sex;
Such from one look in this looking-glass ere you go
    hence,
Such a result so soon—and from such a beginning!

Rather than multiply images of despair in Whitman, I turn to
the most rugged of his self-accusations, in the astonishing "Crossing
Brooklyn Ferry":

It is not upon you alone the dark patches fall,
The dark threw its patches down upon me also,
The best I had done seem'd to me blank and suspicious,
My great thoughts as I supposed them, were they not
    in reality meagre?
Nor is it you alone who know what it is to be evil,
I am he who knew what it was to be evil,
I too knotted the old knot of contrariety,
Blabb'd, blush'd, resented, lied, stole, grudg'd,
Had guile, anger, lust, hot wishes I dared not speak,
Was wayward, vain, greedy, shallow, sly, cowardly,
    malignant,
The wolf, the snake, the hog, not wanting in me,
The cheating look, the frivolous word, the adulterous
    wish, not wanting,
Refusals, hates, postponements, meanness, laziness,
    none of these wanting,
Was one with the rest, the days and haps of the rest,
Was call'd by my nighest name by clear loud voices of

> young men as they saw me approaching or
>   passing,
> Felt their arms on my neck as I stood, or the negligent
>   leaning of their flesh against me as I sat,
> Saw many I loved in the street or ferry-boat or public
>   assembly, yet never told them a word,
> Lived the same life with the rest, the same old
>   laughing, gnawing, sleeping,
> Play'd the part that still looks back on the actor or
>   actress,
> The same old role, the role that is what we make it, as
>   great as we like,
> Or as small as we like, or both great and small.

The barely concealed allusions to Milton's Satan and to *King Lear* strengthen Whitman's catalog of vices and evasions, preparing the poet and his readers for the darker intensities of the great *Sea-Drift* elegies and "Lilacs," poems that are echoed everywhere in Eliot's verse, but particularly in "The Death of Saint Narcissus," *The Waste Land*, and "The Dry Salvages." Many critics have charted these allusions, but I would turn consideration of Eliot's agon with Whitman to the question: "Why Whitman?" It is poetically unwise to go down to the waterline, or go to the headland with Walt Whitman, for then the struggle takes place in an arena where the poet who found his identifying trope in the sea-drift cannot lose.

An answer must be that the belated poet does not choose his trial by landscape or seascape. It is chosen for him by his precursor. Browning's quester in "Childe Roland to the Dark Tower Came" is as overdetermined by Shelley as Eliot is overdetermined by Whitman in *The Waste Land*, which is indeed Eliot's version of "Childe Roland," as it is Eliot's version of Percivale's quest in Tennyson's "The Holy Grail," a poem haunted by Keats in the image of Galahad. "Lilacs" is everywhere in *The Waste Land*: in the very lilacs bred out of the dead land, in the song of the hermit thrush in the pine trees, and most remarkably in the transumption of Whitman walking down to where the hermit thrush sings, accompanied by two companions walking beside him, the thought of death and the knowledge of death:

> Then with the knowledge of death as walking one
>   side of me,

And the thought of death close-walking the other
    side of me,
And I in the middle as with companions, and as
    holding the hands of companions,
I fled forth to the hiding receiving night that talks
    not,
Down to the shores of the water, the path by the
    swamp in the dimness,
To the solemn shadowy cedars and ghostly pines so
    still.

The "crape-veil'd women" singing their dirges through the night for Lincoln are hardly to be distinguished from Eliot's "murmur of maternal lamentation," and Whitman's "tolling tolling bells' perpetual clang" goes on tolling reminiscent bells in *The Waste Land* as it does in "The Dry Salvages." Yet all this is only a first-level working of the influence process, of interest mostly as a return of the repressed. Deeper, almost beyond analytical modes as yet available to criticism, is Eliot's troubled introjection of his nation's greatest and inescapable elegiac poet. "Lilacs" has little to do with the death of Lincoln but everything to do with Whitman's ultimate poetic crisis, beyond which his strongest poetry will cease. *The Waste Land* has little to do with neo-Christian polemics concerning the decline of Western culture, and everything to do with a poetic crisis that Eliot could not quite surmount, in my judgment, since I do not believe that time will confirm the estimate that most contemporary critics have made of *Four Quartets*.

The decisive moment or negative epiphany of Whitman's elegy centers upon his giving up of the tally, the sprig of lilac that is the synecdoche for his image of poetic voice, which he yields up to death and to the hermit thrush's song of death. Eliot's parallel surrender in "What the Thunder Said" is to ask "what have we given?," where the implicit answer is "a moment's surrender," a negative moment in which the image of poetic voice is achieved only as one of Whitman's "retrievements out of the night."

In his essay on Pascal, Eliot says of Montaigne, a little resentfully but with full accuracy, that "he succeeded in giving expression to the skepticism of *every* human being," presumably including Pascal, and Shakespeare, and even T. S. Eliot. What did Whitman succeed in expressing with equal universality? Division between "myself" and "the real me" is surely the answer. Walt Whitman, one of the roughs, an American, is hardly identical with "the Me myself" who:

> Looks with its sidecurved head curious what will come
> next,
> Both in and out of the game, and watching and
> wondering at it.

Thomas Stearns Eliot, looking with side-curved head, both in and out of the game, has little in common with Walt Whitman, one of the roughs, an American, yet almost can be identified with that American "Me myself."

III

The line of descent from Shelley and Keats through Browning and Tennyson to Pound and Eliot would be direct, were it not for the intervention of the genius of the shores of America, the poet of *Leaves of Grass*. Whitman enforces upon Pound and Eliot the American difference, which he had inherited from Emerson, the fountain of our eloquence and of our pragmatism. Most reductively defined, the American poetic difference ensues from a sense of acute isolation, both from an overwhelming space of natural reality, and from an oppressive temporal conviction of belatedness, of having arrived after the event. The inevitable defense against nature is the Gnostic conviction that one is no part of the creation, that one's freedom is invested in the primal abyss. Against belatedness, defense involves an immersion in allusiveness, hardly for its own sake, but in order to reverse the priority of the cultural, pre-American past. American poets from Whitman and Dickinson onwards are more like Milton than Milton is, and so necessarily they are more profoundly Miltonic than even Keats or Tennyson was compelled to be.

What has wasted the land of Eliot's elegiac poem is neither the malady of the Fisher King nor the decline of Christianity, and Eliot's own psychosexual sorrows are not very relevant either. The precursors' strength is the illness of *The Waste Land*; Eliot after all can promise to show us "fear in a handful of dust" only because the monologist of Tennyson's *Maud* already has cried out: "Dead, long dead,/ Long dead!/ And my heart is a handful of dust." Even more poignantly, Eliot is able to sum up all of Whitman's extraordinary "As I Ebb'd with the Ocean of Life" in the single line: "These fragments I have shored against my ruins," where the fragments are not only the verse paragraphs that constitute the text of *The Waste Land*, but crucially are also Whitman's floating sea-drift:

> Me and mine, loose windrows, little corpses,
> Froth, snowy white, and bubbles,
> (See, from my dead lips the ooze exuding at last,
> See, the prismatic colors glistening and rolling,)
> Tufts of straw, sands, fragments,
> Buoy'd hither from many moods, one contradicting
>   another.
> From the storm, the long calm, the darkness, the swell,
> Musing, pondering, a breath, a briny tear, a dab of
>   liquid or soil,
> Up just as much out of fathomless workings fermented
>   and thrown,
> A limp blossom or two, torn, just as much over waves
>   floating, drifted at random,
> Just as much for us that sobbing dirge of Nature,
> Just as much whence we come that blare of the cloud-
>   trumpets,
> We, capricious, brought hither we know not whence,
>   spread out before you,
> You up there walking or sitting,
> Whoever you are, we too lie in drifts at your feet.

"Tufts of straw, sands, fragments" are literally "shored" against Whitman's ruins, as he wends "the shores I know," the shores of America to which, Whitman said, Emerson had led all of us, Eliot included. Emerson's essays, Eliot pugnaciously remarked, "are already an encumbrance," and so they were, and are, and evermore must be for an American writer, but inescapable encumbrances are also stimuli, as Pascal learned in regard to the overwhelming Montaigne.

The Death of Europe

Hugh Kenner

"A Game of Chess" is a convenient place to start our investigations. Chess is played with Queens and Pawns: the set of pieces mimics a social hierarchy, running from "The Chair she sat in, like a burnished throne," to "Goonight Bill. Goonight Lou. Goonight May. Goonight." It is a silent unnerving warfare

> "Speak to me. Why do you never speak. Speak.
> What are you thinking of? What thinking? What?
> I never know what you are thinking. Think."

in which everything hinges on the welfare of the King, the weakest piece on the board, and in this section of the poem invisible (though a "barbarous king" once forced Philomel). Our attention is focused on the Queen.

> The Chair she sat in, like a burnished throne,
> Glowed on the marble, where the glass
> Held up by standards wrought with fruited vines
> From which a golden Cupidon peeped out
> (Another hid his eyes behind his wing)
> Doubled the flames of sevenbranched candelabra
> Reflecting light upon the table as
> The glitter of her jewels rose to meet it,
> From satin cases poured in rich profusion.

From *The Invisible Poet: T. S. Eliot.* © 1959 by Hugh Kenner. Methuen & Co., Ltd., 1959. Originally entitled "The Death of Europe: *The Waste Land.*"

This isn't a Miltonic sentence, brilliantly contorted; it lacks nerve, forgetting after ten words its confident opening ("The Chair she sat in") to dissipate itself among glowing and smouldering sensations, like a progression of Wagner's. Cleopatra "o'erpicturing that Venus where we see / The fancy outwork nature") sat outdoors; this Venusberg interior partakes of "an atmosphere of Juliet's tomb," and the human inhabitant appears once, in a perfunctory subordinate clause. Pope's Belinda conducted "the sacred rites of pride"—

> This casket India's glowing gems unlocks,
> And all Arabia breathes from yonder box.

The woman at the dressing table in *The Waste Land*, implied but never named or attended to, is not like Belinda the moral centre of an innocent dislocation of values but simply the implied sensibility in which these multifarious effects dissolve and find congruence. All things deny nature; the fruited vines are carved, the Cupidons golden, the light not of the sun, the perfumes synthetic, the candelabra (seven-branched, as for an altar) devoted to no rite, the very colour of the firelight perverted by sodium and copper salts. The dolphin is carved, and swims in a "sad light," not, like Antony's delights, "showing his back above the element he lives in."

No will to exploit new sensations is present; the will has long ago died; this opulent ambience is neither chosen nor questioned. The "sylvan scene" is not Eden nor a window but a painting, and a painting of an unnatural event:

> The change of Philomel, by the barbarous king
> So rudely forced; yet there the nightingale
> Filled all the desert with inviolable voice
> And still she cried, and still the world pursues,
> "Jug Jug" to dirty ears.

Her voice alone, like the voice that modulates the thick fluid of this sentence, is "inviolable"; like Tiresias in Thebes, she is prevented from identifying the criminal whom only she can name. John Lyly wrote down her song more than two centuries before Keats (who wasn't interested in what she was saying):

> What bird so sings yet so dos wayle?
> O 'Tis the ravishd Nightingale.

> Jug, Jug, Jug, tereu, shee cryes,
> And still her woes at Midnight rise.
> Brave prick song!

Lyly, not being committed to the idea that the bird was pouring forth its soul abroad, noted that it stuck to its script ("prick song") and himself attempted a transcription. Lyly of course is perfectly aware of what she is trying to say: "tereu" comes very close to "Tereus." It remained for the nineteenth century to dissolve her plight into a symbol of diffuse angst, indeed to impute "ecstasy" amid human desolation, "here, where men sit and hear each other groan"; and for the twentieth century to hang up a painting of the event on a dressing room wall, as pungent sauce to appetites jaded with the narrative clarity of mythologies but responsive to the visceral thrill and the pressures of "significant form." The picture, a "withered stump of time," hangs there, one item in a collection that manages to be not edifying but sinister:

> staring forms
> Leaned out, leaning, hushing the room enclosed.

Then the visitor, as always in Eliot, mounts a stairway—

> Footsteps shuffled on the stair.

—and we get human conversation at last:

> "What is that noise?"
>   The wind under the door.
> "What is that noise now? What is the wind doing?"
>   Nothing again nothing.
>   Do
> You know nothing? Do you see nothing? Do you
>   remember
>   Nothing?"
>   I remember
> Those are pearls that were his eyes.

"My experience falls within my own circle, a circle closed on the outside; and, with all its elements alike, every sphere is opaque to the other which surround it." What is there to say but "nothing"? He remembers a quotation, faintly apposite; in this room the European past, effects and *objets d'art* gathered from many centuries, has suffered a sea-change, into something rich and strange, and stifling. Sensibility here is the very inhibition of life; and activity is reduced to the manic capering of "that Shakespeherian Rag," the past imposing no austerity, existing simply to be used.

> "What shall we do tomorrow?
> What shall we ever do?"
> The hot water at ten.
> And if it rains, a closed car at four.
> And we shall play a game of chess,
> Pressing lidless eyes and waiting for a knock upon the
>   door.

If we move from the queens to the pawns, we find lowlife no more free or natural, equally obsessed with the denial of nature, artificial teeth, chemically procured abortions, the speaker and her interlocutor battening fascinated at secondhand on the life of Lil and her Albert, Lil and Albert interested only in spurious ideal images of one another.

> He'll want to know what you done with that money he
>   gave you
> To get yourself some teeth.
> . . . .
> He said, I swear, I can't bear to look at you.

And this point—nature everywhere denied, its ceremonies simplified to the brutal abstractions of a chess game

> He's been in the army four years, he wants a good time,
> And if you don't give it him, there's others will, I said.
> Oh is there, she said. Something o'that, I said.
> Then I'll know who to thank, she said, and give me a
>   straight look.

—this point is made implicitly by a device carried over from *Whispers of Immortality*, the juxtaposition without comment or copula of two levels of sensibility: the world of one who reads Webster with the world of one who knows Grishkin, the world of the inquiring wind and the sense drowned in odours with the world of ivory teeth and hot gammon. In Lil and Albert's milieu there is fertility, in the milieu where golden Cupidons peep out there is not; but Lil and Albert's breeding betokens not a harmony of wills but only Albert's improvident refusal to leave Lil alone. The chemist with commercial impartiality supplies one woman with "strange synthetic perfumes" and the other with "them pills I took, to bring it off," aphrodisiacs and abortifacients; he is the tutelary deity, uniting the offices of Cupid and Hymen, of a world which is under a universal curse.

From this vantage point we can survey the methods of the first section, which opens with a denial of Chaucer:

> Whan that Aprille with his shoures soote
> The droughte of March hath perced to the roote
> And bathed every veyne in swich licour
> Of which vertu engendred is the flour.
>
> . . . .
>
> Thanne longen folk to goon on pilgrimages.

In the twentieth-century version we have a prayer book heading, "The Burial of the Dead," with its implied ceremonial of dust thrown and of souls reborn; and the poem begins,

> April is the cruellest month, breeding
> Lilacs out of the dead land, mixing
> Memory and desire, stirring
> Dull roots with spring rain.

No "vertu" is engendered amid this apprehensive reaching forward of participles, and instead of pilgrimages we have European tours:

> we stopped in the colonnade,
> And went on in sunlight, into the Hofgarten,
> And drank coffee, and talked for an hour.

Up out of the incantation breaks a woman's voice, giving tongue to the ethnological confusions of the new Europe, the subservience of *partria* to whim of statesmen, the interplay of immutable fact and national pride:

> Bin gar keine Russin, stamm' aus Litauen, echt deutsch.

—a mixing of memory and desire. Another voice evokes the vanished Austro-Hungarian Empire, the inbred malaise of Mayerling, regressive thrills, objectless travels:

> And when we were children, staying at the archduke's,
> My cousin's, he took me out on a sled,
> And I was frightened. He said, Marie,
> Marie, hold on tight. And down we went.
> In the mountains, there you feel free.
> I read, much of the night, and go south in the winter.

"In the mountains, there you feel free." We have only to delete "there" to observe the collapse of more than a rhythm: to observe how the line's exact mimicry of a fatigue which supposes it has reached some ultimate perception can telescope spiritual bankruptcy, deracinated ardour, and an illusion of liberty which is no more than impatience with human society and relief at a temporary change. It was a restless, pointless world that collapsed during the war, agitated out of habit but tired beyond coherence, on the move to avoid itself. The memories in lines 8 and 18 seem spacious and precious now; then, the events punctuated a terrible continuum of boredom.

The plight of the Sibyl in the epigraph rhymes with that of Marie; the terrible thing is to be compelled to stay alive. "For I with these my own eyes have seen the Cumaean Sibyl hanging in a jar; and when the boys said, 'What do you want, Sibyl?' she answered, 'I want to die.' " The sentence is in a macaronic Latin, posterior to the best age, pungently sauced with Greek; Cato would have contemplated with unblinking severity Petronius' readers' jazz-age craving for the cosmopolitan. The Sibyl in her better days answered questions by flinging from her cave handfuls of leaves bearing letters which the postulant was required to arrange in a suitable order; the wind commonly blew half of them away. Like Tiresias, like Philomel, like the modern poet, she divulged forbidden knowledge only in riddles, fitfully. (Tiresias wouldn't answer Oedipus at all; and he put off Odysseus with a puzzle about an oar mistaken for a winnowing fan.) *The Waste Land* is suffused with a functional obscurity, sibylline fragments so disposed as to yield the utmost in connotative power, embracing the fragmented present and reaching back to "that vanished mind of which our mind is a continuation." As for the Sibyl's present exhaustion, she had foolishly asked Apollo for as many years as the grains of sand in her hand; which is one layer in the multilayered line, "I will show you fear in a handful of dust." She is the prophetic power, no longer consulted by heroes but tormented by curious boys, still answering because she must; she is

Madame Sosostris, consulted by dear Mrs. Equitone and harried by police ("One must be so careful these days"); she is the image of the late phase of Roman civilization, now vanished; she is also "the mind of Europe," a mind more important than one's own private mind, a mind which changes but abandons nothing en route, not super-annuating either Shakespeare, or Homer, or the rock drawing of the Magdalenian draughtsmen; but now very nearly exhausted by the effort to stay interested in its own contents.

Which brings us to the "heap of broken images": not only desert ruins of some past from which life was withdrawn with the failure of the water supply, like the Roman cities in North Africa, or Augustine's Carthage, but also the manner in which Shakespeare, Homer, and the drawings of Michelangelo, Raphael, and the Magdalenian draughtsmen coexist in the contemporary cultivated consciousness: fragments, familiar quotations: *poluphloisboio thalasse*, to be or not to be, undo this button, one touch of nature, etc., God creating the Sun and Moon, those are pearls that were his eyes. For one man who knows *The Tempest* intimately there are a thousand who can identify the lines about the cloud-capp'd towers; painting is a miscellany of reproductions, literature a potpourri of quotations, history a chaos of theories and postures (Nelson's telescope, Washington crossing the Delaware, government of, for and by the people, the Colosseum, the guillotine). A desert wind has blown half the leaves away; disuse and vandals have broken the monuments—

> What are the roots that clutch, what branches grow
> Out of this stony rubbish? Son of man,
> You cannot say, or guess, for you know only
> A heap of broken images, where the sun beats,
> And the dead tree gives no shelter, the cricket no relief,
> And the dry stone no sound of water.

Cities are built out of the ruins of previous cities, as *The Waste Land* is built out of the remains of older poems. But at this stage no building is yet in question; the "Son of man" (a portentously generalizing phrase) is moving tirelessly eastward, when the speaker accosts him with a sinister "Come in under the shadow of this red rock," and offers to show him not merely horror and desolation but something older and deeper: fear.

Hence the hyacinth girl, who speaks with urgent hurt simplicity, like the mad Ophelia:

> "You gave me hyacinths first a year ago;
> They called me the hyacinth girl."

They are childlike words, self-pitying, spoken perhaps in memory, perhaps by a ghost, perhaps by a wistful woman now out of her mind. The response exposes many contradictory layers of feeling:

> —Yet when we come back, late, from the Hyacinth
>   garden,
> Your arms full, and your hair wet, I could not
> Speak, and my eyes failed, I was neither
> Living nor dead, and I knew nothing,
> Looking into the heart of light, the silence.

The context is erotic, the language that of mystical experience: plainly a tainted mysticism. "The Hyacinth garden" sounds queerly like a lost cult's sacred grove, and her arms were no doubt full of flowers; what rite was there enacted or evaded we can have no means of knowing.

But another level of meaning is less ambiguous: perhaps in fantasy, the girl has been drowned. Five pages later "A Game of Chess" ends with Ophelia's words before her death; Ophelia gathered flowers before she tumbled into the stream, then lay and chanted snatches of old tunes—

> Frisch weht der Wind
> Der Heimat zu

while her clothes and hair spread out on the waters. "The Burial of the Dead" ends with a sinister dialogue about a corpse in the garden—

> Has it begun to sprout? Will it bloom this year?
> Or has the sudden frost disturbed its bed?

—two Englishmen discussing their tulips, with a note of the terrible intimacy with which murderers imagine themselves being taunted. The traditional British murderer—unlike his American counterpart, who in a vast land instinctively puts distance between himself and the corpse—prefers to keep it near at hand; in the garden, or behind the wainscoting, or

> bones cast in a little low dry garret,
> Rattled by the rat's foot only, year to year.

"The Fire Sermon" opens with despairing fingers clutching and sinking into a wet bank; it closes with Thames-daughters singing from beneath the oily waves. The drowned Phlebas in Section IV varies this theme; and at the close of the poem the response to the last challenge of the thunder alludes to something that happened in a boat:

> your heart would have responded
> Gaily, when invited, beating obedient
> To controlling hands

—but what in fact did happen we are not told; perhaps nothing, or perhaps the hands assumed another sort of control.

In *The Waste Land* as in *The Family Reunion*, the guilt of the protagonist seems coupled with his perhaps imagined responsibility for the fate of a perhaps ideally drowned woman.

> One thinks to escape
> By violence, but one is still alone
> In an over-crowded desert, jostled by ghosts.

(Ghosts that beckon us under the shadow of some red rock)

> It was only reversing the senseless direction
> For a momentary rest on the burning wheel
> That cloudless night in the mid-Atlantic
> When I pushed her over

It must give this man an unusual turn when Madame Sosostris spreads her pack and selects a card as close to his secret as the Tarot symbolism can come:

> Here, said she,
> Is your card, the drowned Phoenician Sailor,
> (Those are pearls that were his eyes. Look!)—

and again:

> this card,
> Which is blank, is something he carries on his back,
> Which I am forbidden to see.

(In what posture did they come back, late, from the Hyacinth Garden, her hair wet, before the planting of the corpse?) It is not clear whether he is comforted to learn that the clairvoyante does not find the Hanged Man.

Hence, then, his inability to speak, his failed eyes, his stunned movement, neither living nor dead and knowing nothing: as Sweeney later puts it,

> He didn't know if he was alive
>   and the girl was dead
> He didn't know if the girl was alive
>   and he was dead
> He didn't know if they both were alive
>   or both were dead.

The heart of light, the silence, seems to be identified with a waste and empty sea, *Oed' und leer das Meer*; so Harry, Lord Monchensey gazed, or thought he remembered gazing, over the rail of the liner:

> You would never imagine anyone could sink so
>   quickly. . . .
> That night I slept heavily, alone. . . .
> I lay two days in contented drowsiness;
> Then I recovered.

He recovered into an awareness of the Eumenides.

At the end of "The Burial of the Dead" it is the speaker's acquaintance Stetson who has planted a corpse in his garden and awaits its fantastic blooming "out of the dead land": whether a hyacinth bulb or a dead mistress there is, in this phantasmagoric cosmos, no knowing. Any man, as Sweeney is to put it,

> has to, needs to, wants to
> Once in a lifetime, do a girl in.

Baudelaire agrees:

> Si le viol, le poison, le poignard, l'incendie,
> N'ont pas encore brodé de leurs plaisants dessins
> Le canevas banal de nos piteux destins,
> C'est que notre âme, hélas! n'est pas assez hardie.

This is from the poem which ends with the line Eliot has appropriated to climax the first section of *The Waste Land*:

> You! hypocrite lecteur!—mon semblable,—mon frère!

Part Two, "A Game of Chess" revolves around perverted nature, denied or murdered offspring; Part Three, "The Fire Sermon," the most explicit of the five sections, surveys with grave denunciatory candour a world of automatic lust, in which those barriers between person and person which so troubled Prufrock are dissolved by the suppression of the person and the transposition of all human needs and desires to a plane of genital gratification.

> The river's tent is broken: the last fingers of leaf
> Clutch and sink into the wet bank. The wind
> Crosses the brown land, unheard. The nymphs
>   are departed.
> Sweet Thames, run softly, till I end my song.

The "tent," now broken would have been composed of the overarching trees that transformed a reach of the river into a tunnel of love; the phrase beckons to mind the broken maidenhead; and a line later the gone harmonious order, by a half-realizable metamorphosis, struggles exhausted an instant against drowning. "The nymphs are departed" both because summer is past, and because the world of Spenser's *Prothalamion* (when nymphs scattered flowers on the water) is gone, if it ever existed except as an ideal fancy of Spenser's.

> The river bears no empty bottles, sandwich papers,
> Silk handkerchiefs, cardboard boxes, cigarette ends
> Or other testimony of summer nights. The
>   nymphs are departed.

From the "brown land," amorists have fled indoors, but the river is not restored to a sixteenth-century purity because the debris of which it is now freed was not a sixteenth-century strewing of petals but a discarding of twentieth-century impedimenta. The nymphs who have this year departed are not the same nymphs who departed in autumns known to Spenser; their friends are "the loitering heirs of city directors," who, unwilling to assume responsibility for any untoward pregnancies,

> Departed, have left no addresses.

Spring will return and bring Sweeney to Mrs. Porter; Mrs. Porter, introduced by the sound of horns and caressed by the moonlight while she laves her feet, is a latter-day Diana bathing; her daughter perhaps, or any of the vanished nymphs, a latter-day Philomel

> So rudely forc'd.
> Tereu.

Next Mr. Eugenides proposes what appears to be a pederastic assignation; and next the typist expects a visitor to her flat.

The typist passage is the great tour de force of the poem; its gentle lyric melancholy, its repeatedly disrupted rhythms, the automatism of its cadences, in alternate lines aspiring and falling nervelessly—

> The time is now propitious, as he guesses,
> The meal is ended, she is bored and tired,
> Endeavours to engage her in caresses
> Which still are unreproved, if undesired.

—constitute Eliot's most perfect liaison between the self-sustaining gesture of the verse and the presented fact. Some twenty-five lines in flawlessly traditional iambic pentameter, alternately rhymed, sustain with their cadenced gravity a moral context in which the dreary business is played out; the texture is lyric rather than dramatic because there is neither doing nor suffering here but rather the mutual compliance of a ritual scene. The section initiates its flow with a sure and perfect line composed according to the best eighteenth-century models:

> At the violet hour, when the eyes and back

which, if the last word were, for instance, "heart," we might suppose to be by a precursor of Wordsworth's. But the harsh sound and incongruous specification of "back" shift us instead to a plane of prosodic disintegration:

> when the eyes and back
> Turn upward from the desk, when the human engine
> waits
> Like a taxi throbbing waiting,

The upturned eyes and back—nothing else, no face, no torso—recall a Picasso distortion; the "human engine" throws pathos down into mechanism. In the next line the speaker for the first time in the poem identifies himself as Tiresias:

> I Tiresias, though blind, throbbing between two lives,
> Old man with wrinkled female breasts, can see

There are three principal stories about Tiresias, all of them relevant. In *Oedipus Rex*, sitting "by Thebes below the wall" he knew why, and as a consequence of what violent death and what illicit amour, the pestilence had fallen on the unreal city, but declined to tell. In the *Odyssey* he "walked among the lowest of the dead" and evaded predicting Odysseus' death by water; the encounter was somehow necessary to Odysseus' homecoming, and Odysseus was somehow satisfied with it, and did get home, for a while. In the *Metamorphoses* he underwent a change of sex for watching the coupling of snakes: presumably the occasion on which he "foresuffered" what is tonight "enacted on this same divan or bed." He is often the prophet who knows but withholds his knowledge, just as Hieronymo, who is mentioned at the close of the poem, knew how the tree he had planted in his garden came to bear his dead son, but was compelled to withhold that knowldge until he could write a play which, like *The Waste Land*, employs several languages and a framework of allusions impenetrable to anyone but the "hypocrite lecteur." It is an inescapable shared guilt that makes us so intimate with the contents of this strange deathly poem; it is also, in an age that has eaten of the tree of the knowledge of psychology and anthropology ("After such knowledge, what forgiveness?"), an inescapable morbid sympathy with everyone else, very destructive to the coherent personality, that (like Tiresias' years as a woman) enables us to join with him in "foresuffering all." These sciences afford us an *illusion* of understanding other people, on which we build sympathies that in an ideal era would have gone out with a less pathological generosity, and that are as likely as not projections of our self-pity and self-absorption, vices for which Freud and Frazer afford dangerous nourishment. Tiresias is he who has lost the sense of other people as inviolably other, and who is capable neither of pity nor terror but only of a fascination spuriously related to compassion, which is merely the twentieth century's special mutation of indifference. Tiresias can see

> At the violet hour, the evening hour that strives
> Homeward, and brings the sailor home from sea,
> The typist home at teatime, clears her breakfast, lights
> Her stove, and lays out food in tins.

Syntax, like his sensibility and her routine, undergoes total collapse. A fine throbbing line intervenes:

> Out of the window perilously spread

and bathos does not wholly overtopple the completing Alexandrine:

> Her drying combinations touched by the sun's last rays.

"Combinations" sounds a little finer than the thing it denotes; so does "divan":

> On the divan are piled (at night her bed)
> Stockings, slippers, camisoles and stays.

Some transfiguring word touches with glory line after line:

> He, the young man carbuncular, arrives,

If he existed, and if he read those words, how must he have marvelled at the alchemical power of language over his inflamed skin! As their weary ritual commences, the diction alters; it moves to a plane of Johnsonian dignity without losing touch with them; they are never "formulated, sprawling on a pin."

"Endeavours to engage her in caresses" is out of touch with the small house agent's clerk's speech, but it is such a sentence as he might *write*; Eliot has noted elsewhere how "an artisan who can talk the English language beautifully while about his work or in a public bar, may compose a letter painfully written in a dead language bearing some resemblance to a newspaper leader and decorated with words like 'maelstrom' and 'pandemonium.' " So it is with the diction of this passage: it reflects the words with which the participants might clothe, during recollection in tranquillity, their own notion of what they have been about, presuming them capable of such self-analysis; and it maintains simultaneously Tiresias' fastidious impersonality. The rhymes come with a weary inevitability that parodies the formal elegance of Gray; and the episode modulates at its close into a key to which Goldsmith can be transposed:

> When lovely woman stoops to folly and
> Paces about her room again, alone,
> She smoothes her hair with automatic hand,
> And puts a record on the gramophone.

With her music and her lures "perilously spread" she is a London siren; the next line, "This music crept by me upon the water," if it is lifted from the *Tempest*, might as well be adapted from the twelfth book of the *Odyssey*.

After the Siren, the violated Thames-daughters, borrowed from Wagner, the "universal artist" whom the French Symbolists delighted to honour. The opulent Wagnerian pathos, with its harmonic rather than linear development and its trick of entrancing the attention with leitmotifs, is never unrelated to the methods of *The Waste Land*. One of the characters in "A Dialogue on Dramatic Poetry," though he has railed at Wagner as "pernicious," yet would not willingly resign his experience of Wagner; for Wagner had more than a bag of orchestral tricks and a corrupt taste for mythologies, he had also an indispensable sense of his own age, something that partly sustains and justifies his methods. "A sense of his own age"—the ability to "recognize its pattern while the pattern was yet incomplete"—was a quality Eliot in 1930 was to ascribe to Baudelaire. One who has possessed it cannot simply be ignored, though he is exposed to the follies of his age as well as sensitive to its inventions. At the very least he comes to symbolize a phase in "the mind of Europe" otherwise difficult to locate or name; at best, his methods, whether or not they merited his own fanaticism, are of permanent value to later artists for elucidating those phases of human sensibility to the existence of which they originally contributed. This principle is quite different from the academic or counteracademic notion that art must be deliberately adulterated because its preoccupations are.

Wagner, more than Frazer or Miss Weston, presides over the introduction into *The Waste Land* of the Grail motif. In Wagner's opera, the Sangreal quest is embedded in an opulent and depraved religiosity, as in Tennyson's *Holy Grail* the cup, "rose-red, with beatings in it, as if alive, till all the white walls of my cell were dyed with rosy colours leaping on the wall," never succeeds in being more than the reward of a refined and sublimated erotic impulse. Again Eliot notes of Baudelaire that "in much romantic poetry the sadness is due to the exploitation of the fact that no human relations are adequate to human desires, but also to the disbelief in any further object for human desires than that which, being human, fails to satisfy them." The Grail was in mid-nineteenth-century art an attempt to postulate such an object; and the quest for that vision unites the poetry of baffled sadness to "the poetry of flight," a genre which Eliot distinguishes in quoting Baudelaire's "Quand partons-nous vers le bonheur?" and characterizes as "a dim recognition of the direction of beatitude."

So in Part V of *The Waste Land* the journey eastward among the red rocks and heaps of broken images is fused with the journey to Emmaus ("He who was living is now dead. We who were living are now dying") and the approach to the Chapel Perilous.

The quester arrived at the Chapel Perilous had only to ask the meaning of the things that were shown him. Until he has asked their meaning, they have none; after he has asked, the king's wound is healed and the waters commence again to flow. So in a civilization reduced to "a heap of broken images" all that is requisite is sufficient curiosity; the man who asks what one or another of these fragments means—seeking, for instance, "a first-hand opinion about Shakespeare"—may be the agent of regeneration. The past exists in fragments precisely because nobody cares what it meant; it will unite itself and come alive in the mind of anyone who succeeds in caring, who is unwilling that Shakespeare shall remain the name attached only to a few tags everyone half-remembers, in a world where "we know too much, and are convinced of too little."

Eliot develops the nightmare journey with consummate skill, and then manœuvres the reader into the position of the quester, presented with a terminal heap of fragments which it is his business to inquire about. The protagonist in the poem perhaps does not inquire; they are fragments he has shored against his ruins. Or perhaps he does inquire; he has at least begun to put them to use, and the "arid plain" is at length behind him.

The journey is prepared for by two images of asceticism: the brand plucked from the burning, and the annihilation of Phlebas the Phoenician. "The Fire Sermon," which opens by Thames water, closes with a burning, a burning that images the restless lusts of the nymphs, the heirs of city directors, Mr. Eugenides, the typist and the young man carbuncular, the Thames-daughters. They are unaware that they burn. "I made no comment. What should I resent?" They burn nevertheless, as the protagonist cannot help noticing when he shifts his attention from commercial London to commercial Carthage (which stood on the North African shore, and is now utterly destroyed). There human sacrifices were dropped into the furnaces of Moloch, in a frantic gesture of appeasement. There Augustine burned with sensual fires: "a cauldron of unholy loves sang all about mine ears"; and he cried, "O Lord, Thou pluckest me out." The Buddhist ascetic on the other hand does not ask to be plucked out; he simply turns away from the senses because (as the Buddhist Fire Sermon states) they are each of them on fire. As for Phlebas the Phoenician, a trader sailing perhaps to Britain, his asceticism is enforced: "A current under sea picked his bones in whispers," he forgets the benisons of sense, "the cry of gulls and the deep sea swell" as well as "the profit and loss," and he spirals down, like Dante's

Ulysses, through circling memories of his age and youth, "as Another chose." (An account of a shipwreck, imitated from the Ulysses episode in Dante, was one of the long sections deleted from the original *Waste Land*.) Ulysses in hell was encased in a tongue of flame, death by water having in one instance secured not the baptismal renunciation of the Old Adam, but an eternity of fire. Were there some simple negative formula for dealing with the senses, suicide would be the sure way to regeneration.

Part V opens, then, in Gethsemane, carries us rapidly to Golgotha, and then leaves us to pursue a nightmare journey in a world now apparently deprived of meaning.

> Here is no water but only rock
> Rock and no water and the sandy road
> The road winding above among the mountains
> Which are mountains of rock without water
> If there were water we should stop and drink.

The whirling, obsessive reduplication of single words carries the travellers through a desert, through the phases of hallucination in which they number phantom companions, and closes with a synoptic vision of the destruction of Jerusalem ("Murmur of maternal lamentation" obviously recalling "daughters of Jerusalem, weep not for me, but for yourselves and your children") which becomes *sub specie aeternitatis* the destruction by fire of civilization after civilization.

> Jerusalem Athens Alexandria
> Vienna London
> Unreal.

The woman at the dressing table recurs:

> A woman drew her long black hair out tight
> And fiddled whisper music on those strings;

her "golden Cupidons" are transmogrified:

> And bats with baby faces in the violet light
> Whistled, and beat their wings
> And crawled head downward down a blackened wall

and where towers hang "upside down in air" stability is imaged by a deserted chapel among the mountains, another place from which the life has gone but in which the meaning is latent, awaiting only

a pilgrim's advent. The cock crows as it did when Peter wept tears
of penitence; as in *Hamlet*, it disperses the night spirits.

> Then a damp gust
> Bringing rain.

There the activity of the protagonist ends. Some forty remaining lines
in the past tense recapitulate the poem in terms of the oldest wisdom
accessible to the West. The thunder's DA is one of those primordial
Indo-European roots that recur in the *Oxford Dictionary*, a random
leaf of the Sibyl's to which a thousand derivative words, now automatic currency, were in their origins so many explicit glosses. If the
race's most permanent wisdom is its oldest, then DA, the voice of the
thunder and of the Hindu sages, is the cosmic voice not yet dissociated
into echoes. It underlies the Latin infinitive "dare," and all its Romance derivatives; by a sound change, the Germanic "geben," the
English "give." It is the root of "datta," "dayadhvam," "damyata":
give, sympathize, control: three sorts of giving. To sympathize is to
give oneself; to control is to give governance.

> Then spoke the thunder
> DA
> *Datta*: what have we given?
> My friend, blood shaking my heart
> The awful daring of a moment's surrender
> Which an age of prudence can never retract
> By this, and this only, we have existed.

The first surrender was our parents' sexual consent; and when we
are born again it is by a new surrender, inconceivable to the essentially
satiric sensibility with which a Gerontion contemplates

> De Bailhache, Fresca, Mrs. Cammel, whirled
> Beyond the circuit of the shuddering Bear,

and requiring a radical modification of even a Tiresias' negative
compassion.

> The awful daring of a moment's surrender
> . . . .
> Which is not to be found in our obituaries
> Or in memories draped by the beneficent spider
> Or under seals broken by the lean solicitor
> In our empty rooms.

The lean solicitor, like the inquiring worm, breaks seals that in life-time were held prissily inviolate; the will he is about to read registers not things given but things abandoned. The thunder is telling us what Tiresias did not dare tell Oedipus, the reason for the universal curse: "What have we given?" As for "Dayadhvam," "sympathize":

> DA
> *Dayadhvam*: I have heard the key
> Turn in the door once and turn once only
> We think of the key, each in his prison
> Thinking of the key, each confirms a prison

—a prison of inviolate honour, self-sufficiency, like that in which Coriolanus locked himself away. Coriolanus' city was also under a curse, in which he participated. His energies sufficed in wartime (Eliot's poem was written three years after the close of the Great War), but in peacetime it becomes clear that "he did it to please his mother, and to be partly proud." He is advised to go through the forms of giving and sympathy, but

> [Not] by the matter which your heart prompts you,
> But with such words that are but rooted in
> Your tongue.

After his banishment he goes out "like to a lonely dragon," and plots the destruction of Rome. His final threat is to stand

> As if a man were author of himself
> And knew no other kin.

He is an energetic and purposeful Prufrock, concerned with the figure he cuts and readily humiliated; Prufrock's radical fault is not his lack of energy and purpose. Coriolanus is finally shattered like a statue; and if

> Only at nightfall, aethereal rumours
> Revive for a moment a broken Coriolanus,

it may be only as the Hollow Men in Death's dream kingdom hear voices "in the wind's singing," and discern sunlight on a broken column. Do the rumours at nightfall restore him to momentary life, or restore his memory to the minds of other self-sufficient unsym-pathizing men?

> DA
> *Damyata*: The boat responded
> Gaily, to the hand expert with sail and oar
> The sea was calm, your heart would have responded
> Gaily, when invited, beating obedient
> To controlling hands.

Unlike the rider, who may dominate his horse, the sailor survives and moves by cooperation with a nature that cannot be forced; and this directing, sensitive hand, feeling on the sheet the pulsation of the wind and on the rudder the momentary thrust of waves, becomes the imagined instrument of a comparably sensitive human relationship. If dominance compels response, control invites it; and the response comes "gaily." But—"would have": the right relationship was never attempted.

> I sat upon the shore
> Fishing, with the arid plain behind me.

The journey eastward across the desert is finished; though the king's lands are waste, he has arrived at the sea.

> Shall I at least set my lands in order?

Isaiah bade King Hezekiah set his lands in order because he was destined not to live; but Candide resolved to cultivate his own garden as a way of living. We cannot set the whole world in order; we can rectify ourselves. And we are destined to die, but such order as lies in our power is nevertheless desirable.

> London Bridge is falling down falling down falling
> down
> *Poi s'ascose nel foco che gli affina*
> *Quando fiam uti chelidon*—O swallow swallow
> *Le Prince d'Aquitaine à la tour abolie*
> These fragments I have shored against my ruins.

An English nursery rhyme, a line of Dante's, a scrap of the late Latin *Pervigilium Veneris*, a phrase of Tennyson's ("O swallow, swallow, could I but follow") linked to the fate of Philomel, an image from a pioneer nineteenth-century French visionary who hanged himself on a freezing January morning: "a heap of broken images," and a fragmentary conspectus of the mind of Europe. Like the Knight in the Chapel Perilous, we are to ask what these relics mean; and the answers will lead us into far recesses of tradition.

The history of London Bridge (which was disintegrating in the eighteenth century, and which had symbolized, with its impractical houses, a communal life now sacrificed to abstract transportation—

> A crowd flowed over London Bridge, so many,
> I had not thought death had undone so many.)

is linked by the nursery rhyme with feudal rituals ("gold and silver, my fair lady") and festivals older still. Dante's line focuses the tradition of Christian asceticism, in which "burning" is voluntarily undergone. Dante's speaker was a poet:

> Ieu sui Arnaut, que plor e vau cantan;
> Consiros vei la passada folor,
> E vei jausen lo jorn, que'esper, denan.

"Consiros vei la passada folor": compare "With the arid plain behind me." "Vau cantan": he goes singing in the fire, like the children in the Babylonian furnace, not quite like Philomel whose song is pressed out of her by the memory of pain. The *Pervigilium Veneris* is another rite, popular, postpagan, pre-Christian, welcoming in the spring and inciting to love: "Cras amet qui numquam amavit"; he who has never loved, let him love tomorrow; secular love, but its trajectory leads, via the swallow, aloft. Tennyson's swallow nearly two thousand years later ("Could I but follow") flies away from an earthbound poet, grounded in an iron time, and meditating "la poésie des départs." That poem is a solo, not a folk ritual. As for the Prince of Aquitaine with the ruined tower, he is one of the numerous personae Gérard de Nerval assumes in *El Desdichado*: "Suis-je Amour ou Phébus, Lusignan ou Biron?" as the speaker of *The Waste Land* is Tiresias, the Phoenician Sailor, and Ferdinand Prince of Naples. He has lingered in the chambers of the sea

> J'ai rêvé dans la grotte où nage la sirène

and like Orpheus he has called up his love from the shades:

> Et j'ai deux fois vainqueur traversé l'Achéron
> Modulant tour à tour sur la lyre d'Orphée
> Les soupirs de la sainte et les cris de la fée.

So *The Waste Land* contains Augustine's cries and the song of the Thames-daughters; but de Nerval, the pioneer Symbolist, is enclosed in a mood, in a poetic state, surrounded by his own symbols ("Je suis le ténébreux,—le veuf,—l'inconsolé"), offering to a remembered order, where the vine and the rose were one, only the supplication of a dead man's hand, "Dans la nuit du tombeau," where "ma seule étoile est morte": under the twinkle of a fading star. It is some such state as his, these images suggest, that is to be explored in "The Hollow Men"; he inhabits death's dream kingdom. The mind of Europe, some time in the nineteenth century, entered an uneasy phase of sheer dream.

> These fragments I have shored against my ruins
> Why then Ile fit you. Hieronymo's mad againe.

Here Eliot provides us with a final image for all that he has done: his poem is like Hieronymo's revenge play. Hieronymo's enemies— the public for the poet in our time—commission an entertainment:

> It pleased you,
> At the entertainment of the ambassador,
> To grace the king so much as with a show.
> Now, were your study so well furnished,
> As for the passing of the first night's sport
> To entertain my father with the like
> Or any such-like pleasing motion,
> Assure yourself, it would content them well.
> HIER: Is this all?
> BAL.:   Ay, this is all.
> HIER: Why then, I'll fit you. Say no more.
> When I was young, I gave my mind
> And plied myself to fruitless poetry;
> Which though it profit the professor naught,
> Yet is it passing pleasing to the world.

It profits the professor naught, like Philomel's gift of song; and pleases those who have no notion of what it has cost, or what it will ultimately cost them. Hieronymo goes on to specify:

> Each one of us
> Must act his part in unknown languages,
> That it may breed the more variety:

> As you, my Lord, in Latin, I in Greek,
> You in Italian, and for because I know
> That Bellimperia hath practised the French,
> In courtly French shall all her phrases be.

Each of these languages occurs in *The Waste Land*; all but Greek, in the list of shored fragments. Balthasar responds, like a critic in *The New Statesman*,

> But this will be a mere confusion,
> And hardly shall we all be understood.

Hieronymo, however, is master of his method:

> It must be so: for the conclusion
> Shall prove the invention and all was good.

Hieronymo's madness, in the context provided by Eliot, is that of the Platonic bard. If we are to take the last two lines of *The Waste Land* as the substance of what the bard in his sibylline trance has to say, then the old man's macaronic tragedy appears transmuted into the thunder's three injunctions, Give, Sympathize, Control, and a triple "Peace," "repeated as here," says the note, "a formal ending to an Upanishad."

Imagism and Its Consequences

Graham Hough

The years between 1910 and the second world war saw a revolution in the literature of the English language as momentous as the Romantic one of a century before. It is an Anglo-American development that is itself part of a whole European affair. Beside the names of Yeats, Joyce, Eliot and Pound we should wish to place those of Gide, Valéry and Thomas Mann, perhaps Proust and Rilke from an earlier generation. Here is our identification parade for the modern spirit in letters. But here, too, we have such a huge and various collective phenomenon that almost anything we care to say about it would be true of some part or other; the target is so large that any chance-aimed shot would be sure to hit it somewhere. If we look at it *en masse* we shall soon find ourselves speaking of crisis in Western values, of dissociation of sensibility, of alienation, and disinherited minds. Looking from this vertiginous height we shall surely be able to make many observations that are true, the more easily since they are not liable to the contradictions of particularity. Let us descend and recover balance by observing a fixed spot—London in the years just before 1914. It was there that the English cell of an almost world-wide poetic conspiracy was being incubated—the first plot against the literary establishment for over a hundred years. Of course foreign agents were at work; there had been correspondence with France and the Orient; a person from Idaho and one from St. Louis were actually present.

From *Reflections on a Literary Revolution*. © 1960 by Catholic University of America, Inc. Catholic University of America Press, 1960.

So in the next few years "modern poetry" came into being. Strangely, it is still modern poetry, the same article, sold under the same name. The revolution is long past. Of the central revolutionary quartet—Pound, Eliot, Joyce and Wyndham Lewis—"the men of 1914," as Lewis liked to call them (it is characteristic that the turn of phrase should be borrowed from European revolutionary politics) two are dead, one legally irresponsible, and the fourth is happily still with us, the greatest living man of letters [essay first published 1960]. A generation has had to pass to bring about this change of aspect. But nothing has happened to dispute with their productions the title of modern letters. No avant-garde had advanced any farther. There is no avant-garde. When I was a boy "modern poetry" was to be distinguished from poetry simple. Poetry was inherited from parents and learnt at school; it was the "Ode on a Grecian Urn" and "The Solitary Reaper." Modern poetry was read in a different context; neither one's parents nor anyone at school knew anything about it. Modern poetry is now academically respectable. It is taught in college courses, and the exposition of it gives employment to many worthy persons. But it is still almost as distinct from "poetry" as ever. Distinct in the general imagination, and not only in that; even among those who seriously profess the arts there is a feeling of the discontinuity between the literature of our century and that of any previous one. The singularity of modern poetry, for example, is one of the arguments used by C. S. Lewis to support his hypothesis of a great rift in our culture just before the present age.

This consciousness of modernity is a distinctively modern thing; it is largely the work of the revolutionary generation itself. Pound's essays were called *Make It New*. In the stream of advice and exhortation he offered to young writers there is a continual insistence on novelty and on being up-to-date. "No good poetry is ever written in a manner twenty years old." "The scientist does not expect to be acclaimed as a great scientist until he has *discovered* something." In both his and Eliot's criticism we are always hearing about "what remains to be done," "what is to be done next." A curious instance of this acute period-consciousness occurs quite recently, in Mr. Eliot's introduction to Pound's *Literary Essays*. He cites as one of the tricks of malevolent critics—"to quote what a writer said twenty or thirty years ago as if it was something he had said yesterday." It is hard to imagine Johnson or Coleridge or Arnold finding it "malevolent" to quote a twenty-year-old dictum without the appropriate date. Lest I be suspected of malevolence may I add that the date of [Eliot's] remark is 1954, a date far removed from the dust of revolutionary conflict. Plainly the instigators of the late poetic innovation were badly frightened by a Zeitgeist, and the effects have been lasting.

The new poetry was new in the twenties, and it is still new, in the sense that we have nothing newer. As early as 1935 we find Sir Herbert Read, in an essay called *Form in Modern Poetry*, complaining of backsliding, of a decline in revolutionary and experimental ardour. It might be that the new tradition had established itself, that we now have a body of followers working in an accepted mode. But this is not true, or true only in a very restricted area. The revolution of 1914 was quite as momentous as the Romantic one of over a century before, but it was different. The Romantic change was not at all antipathetic to ancient and deep-rooted tendencies. In many ways it was a return to them; the old textbook term is after all the Romantic Revival. The result is that its habits of feeling and expression are a model for the next hundred years. The nineteenth-century shelves are stuffed with Wordsworthian poems, Keatsian poems and Byronic poems. The modern revolution has had a different fate. In one direction, in the establishment of a modern colloquial poetic idiom, the younger writers have certainly learnt the lesson of their elder contemporaries. All that purgation of poetic diction that has been so carefully and beautifully worked out, both in theory and in practice, by Mr. Eliot has become an almost absolute critical rule. The rule has been formulated, with something less than complete approval, in a recent essay by John Crowe Ransom: "That is simply a bad poem whose unfashionable or dated diction the plain reader spots at the first reading." But other parts of the newly conquered territory are being little cultivated. A belated critical posse in full jungle kit still hacks its way through these no longer very forbidding areas, in the pages of the semiacademic reviews; and that is about all. The influence of the generation of 1914 was always of a peculiar kind. On taste, ideas and feelings about literature it was dynamic, radical, and in the end largely triumphant. A diluted version of Mr. Eliot's critical doctrine (and that includes, at one remove, a great deal of the doctrines of Hulme, Pound and Lewis) is by now the possession of undergraduates and schoolboys. Mr. Eliot's version of English literary history is as much an orthodoxy as Matthew Arnold's was a generation before. Yet the direct effect on literary practice has been strangely small. There is no other poem of any significance remotely like *The Waste Land*; the metrics and the ordonnance of Pound's *Propertius* have had no successors whatever; no one has ever seriously attempted to emulate Joyce's most characteristic experiments; and the extraordinary bundle of detestations that go to make up Wyndham Lewis are so arbitrary that they are a monument to nothing but himself.

A rich and vigorous body of literature has established itself, but has not established a workable tradition. A possibility (it has been faintly entertained by Mr. [R. P.] Blackmur) is that it is not through this self-consciously "modern" literature that the main road runs; that these writers are not the transmitters of the most vigorous poetic life of our time. Perhaps the authentic torch has been borne by writers of a more traditional cast—shall we say by Robert Frost, Robert Graves and E. M. Forster? But this is not really a possibility. It is not the admirable workers in traditional modes who have given the twentieth century its peculiar kind of vitality. The suggestion is entertained only to be dismissed. As I show it to the door I become aware of one of its relatives faintly demanding admittance. Deep in the folk-memory of English literary critics is the echo of a time when it was possible to speak of something called "the English spirit." Few, in a state of full vigilance, would allow this faded trope to escape their lips now. But I intend to employ it not meaning whatever Sir Arthur Quiller-Couch would have meant by it but meaning something like the spirit of the language, the whole drift and pressure given by the whole body of poetry written in English. The suggestion that knocks at the door is that specifically "modern" poetry is hostile to this spirit and has tried to move against that pressure. A few very powerful talents succeeded in establishing idiosyncratic positions. No one since has been powerful enough to take up the same stance or sufficiently supple and adaptable to go back and take up the old path where it left off. This is at least plausible as far as English is concerned, though in America it may be less so. It need not surprise us when we consider that two of the "men of 1914" were Americans, one an Irishman, and the origins of the other shrouded in mystery.

The suggestion may be allowed to stand in the doorway, for we are not yet in a position to examine its credentials. We have not yet asked what the nature of the twentieth-century revolution is, so we cannot yet know how it is related to the English poetic tradition. It is notable that whatever was happening in those years has not yet acquired a name. . . .

If we look into the archives of the period of revolutionary preparation, the name that is going about is Imagism. . . . In the narrow sense, the name refers to a movement whose history was brief, broken and querulous, whose poetic results were minuscule. The refinement of our numbers was to be accomplished by the introduction of the *haiku*, the Japanese poem of seventeen syllables. The tongue that Milton spake is not easily compressed into seventeen-syllable units; and even in its longer flights Imagism remains a small affair. But as a centre and an influence it is not small. It is the hard irreducible core of a whole cluster of poetic ideas that extend far beyond Imagism as a movement. Imagist ideas are at the centre of the characteristic poetic procedures of our time, and there is a case for giving the word a wider extension.

Imagism sounds like a by-blow from Symbolism. Image and symbol—we have been pestered by both words long enough; often we do not distinguish between them. If we were talking about continental Europe instead of the Anglo-American literary world there would be no need to make much play with Imagism. Symbolism is already there, well established and more or less understood. There have been several attempts to see the new poetry in English simply as a part of this earlier European movement. . . . However, there is room for a distinction here, and not only room, but a real need for it.

Though Symbolism is in a sense a late development of Romantic thought it takes a decisively new turn. The great Romantic writers (Wordsworth, Coleridge, Keats) all see literature as deeply rooted in experience. The confessional poem, the truth that has been "proved upon our pulses," the attitude of those "to whom the miseries of the world are misery and will not let them rest"—these are its characteristic expressions. Symbolism moves in the direction of an autonomous art, severed from life and experience by an impassable gulf. The Symbolists share with the Romantics the reliance on the epiphany, the moment of revelation; but they differ sharply about its status in nature and its relation to art. Wordsworth's spiritual life is founded on such moments of illumination, and it is the business of his poetry both to describe them and to relate them to the whole experience of a long ordered lifetime. For the Symbolist poet there is no question of describing an experience; the moment of illumination only occurs in its embodiment in some particular artistic form. There is no question of relating it to the experience of a lifetime, for it is unique, it exists in the poem alone. Rimbaud's *alchimie du verbe* is not a mere phrase, for the poet not only transmits, he creates the revelations that make up his world.

Symbolism therefore has strong transcendental overtones. The poet is a magus, calling reality into existence. Or he is the sole transmitter of a mysterious system of correspondences that actually pervades the universe but only becomes apparent in art. Or he is capable of evoking from the *Anima Mundi* symbols of the profoundest import, but strictly unexpoundable, for their content is inseparable from the form of their first expression. At times we seem to be in something like the medieval symbolic universe. But that symbolism has a key, a key given once and for all in revelation. Since the means of grace and some means of instruction are available to all, it was in a sense a joy in widest commonalty spread; while the Symbolist universe reveals itself only in glimpses, only in art, and only to initiates.

Now while modern literature has been afflicted with a persistent hangover from the rich Symbolist symposium, the magical and transcendental pretensions of Symbolism have almost entirely disappeared. It is only in the work of the early Yeats that we can find the Symbolist doctrine in full bloom. Even here it is considerably contaminated with a nonliterary occultism—theosophy, spiritualism, Madame Blavatsky and the order of the Golden Dawn. It is doubtful whether we can properly speak of a Symbolist movement in English poetry, in a historical sense. Of course, if we like to take Symbolism as a universal, recurrent phenomenon we can rope in such diverse figures as Blake and Herman Melville, and no doubt a dozen others, and make some use of the concept. I am speaking of Symbolism as a more or less dateable historical development, as the term is used in French literature. This development several times looks as though it is going to occur in English, but it never comes to much, though relations with the French movement were frequent and beguiling. There was a foreshadowing of French Symbolism in the Pre-Raphaelites; there were many importations of Symbolist doctrine in the nineties; but it is not until the years before the first world war that French doctrines and practice showed signs of giving rise to a new poetry in England.

The history is complicated, and it has still only partly been written. There are probably many reasons that Symbolism took such feeble roots in England. We had a little of it of our own already; English poetry lacks a Baudelaire to stand as *éminence grise* behind the movement; above all, Symbolist influence on sensibility was not paralleled by a close study of Symbolist forms. The fin de siècle, fertile in sentiments and attitudes that are important for modern literature, was curiously powerless to find forms to match them; and it was not until the years around 1910 that a radically new poetry, and that implies a new poetic form, really begins to appear in English. In those years, when the group that were later to call themselves Imagists were laying their plans, the transcendental pretensions of Symbolism were no longer easy to entertain. The career of Mallarmé had ended in silence and something like despair. *Un coup de dès jamais n'abolira le hasard.* Rimbaud's defection to slave trading in Africa was itself a symbol of the inefficacy of magical Symbolism; and the innocuous chastities of Japanese poetry in dilute translation were focussing attention on the surface properties rather than on the mystic attributes of the symbol.

Certain aspects of Symbolist doctrine persist, but the nature of the attention is changed. Revelation becomes technique, incantation becomes a code of prohibitions. What emerges is a new phenomenon, to which we rightly give a new name—Imagism. Not to deal in definition at this stage, and in the hope that things will become clearer as we go on, we can describe it roughly as Symbolism without the magic. The symbol, naked and unexplained, trailing no clouds of glory, becomes the image. . . . No transparent envelopes, or mysterious absences, or invisible essences. Direct treatment of the *thing*, we are told, is the great object. T. E. Hulme's early criticism hammers away at accurate description, hardness, clarity. And we know what came of it:

> The apparition of these faces in the crowd;
> Petals on a wet, black bough.
>
> [Ezra Pound]

Those dozens of little poems in Pound's *Ripostes* and later; clear, limited, without resonance, without transparency. "The natural object is always the adequate symbol"—but of what? Of nothing but itself. A world composed of atomic notations, each image separate from all the others. They neither lead into each other nor to apprehension on any other level. There is in all Pound's practice and theory at this time a positivism, a defiant insistence on the surface of things, and an insistence that the surface of things is all.

Pound writes of Laurent Tailhade:

> I think this sort of clear presentation is of the noblest tra-
> dition of our craft. It is surely the scourge of fools. It is
> what may be called the "prose tradition" of poetry, and
> by this I mean that it is a practice of speech common to
> good prose and good verse alike. . . . It means constatation
> of fact. It presents. It does not comment. . . . It is not a
> criticism of life. I mean it does not deal in opinion. It
> washes its hands of theories. It does not attempt to justify
> anybody's ways to anybody or anything else.

But even Pound could not consistently maintain that the clear presentation of the object was the sole aim of poetry. Though he often
talks in T. E. Hulme's terms, as though presentational accuracy was
an end in itself, in other places the natural object is seen as the
equivalent of an emotion. Poetry is the art of making equations for
emotions. But it is an equation of which one side only is to be
presented. Imagist convention forbids that most ancient recipe for a
poem—the poem in which first a natural object is presented, and
then some reflection on human experience that arises from it, or is
in some way parallel to it. As a student of Provençal Pound must
have been familiar with the *reverdie* and its long history—the spring
song, whose first stanza presents "the soote sesoun that bud and
bloom forth brings," whose later ones present the happy love that
resembles it, or the unhappy love that contrasts with it. By his
subsequent lights it is only possible for the poet to say "It is Spring"—
and, unspoken, on no account to be uttered, only to be understood—
"if you care to make any deductions from this to my state of mind,
you may." But since the natural object is always the adequate symbol
the poem will not make itself responsible for any of these deductions.

> I leaned against a sturdy oak,
> I thought it was a trusty tree;
> But first it bent and syne it broke,
> Sae did my true love lichtly me.

This is too explicit for true Imagist principles. The proper procedure
is to be seen in Pound's "Fan-Piece for her Imperial Lord":

> O fan of white silk,
>   clear as the frost on the grass-blade,
> You also are laid aside.

So far, merely a change of rhetorical convention; a laconic novelty of procedure that has its own charm. We know well enough what the Imagists are tired of. They are tired of Arnold's "Dover Beach"; the extended picture of the moonlight, the beach and the tide; and then the inevitable, the too-long expected "The sea of faith was once too at the full . . . "; the melancholy nineteenth-century automatism by which no natural object can appear without trailing its inglorious little cloud of moralising behind it. They were right to be tired. One aspect of the history of poetry is an intermittent warfare against automatisms, clichés of feeling and expression. Only an intermittent warfare, for there are long periods when poetry can rest, contented, healthy and active, within a set of received conventions. But these periods come to an end. This was a time when the battlefront had again become particularly active.

From this point of view Imagism was good tactics, and the skirmish was conducted with vigour and address. But tactics are not principles, and there is always danger when they are erected into principles. Pound was particularly liable to make this transformation. His insistence on procedure and technique is the beginning of this. "A few don'ts"; as though the writing of poetry is the adroit employment of a series of gimmicks; the continual invocation of "the expert"; the deference (in writing that shows little deference) to the progress of the natural sciences;

> What the expert is tired of to-day the public will be tired of to-morrow.
>
> It is not necessary that a poem should rely on its music, but if it does rely on its music that music must be such as will delight the expert.
>
> The scientist does not expect to be acclaimed as a great scientist until he has *discovered* something. He begins by learning what has been discovered already. He goes from that point onward.
>
> The best history of literature, more particularly of poetry, would be a twelve-volume anthology in which each poem was chosen . . . because it contained an invention, a definite contribution to the art of verbal expression.

When Imagist doctrine was reinforced by Pound's study (if it can be called study) of Chinese, and his understanding (which was a misunderstanding) of the nature of Chinese ideogram, the gimmicks were well on the way to becoming a principle. When Pound took over Fenollosa's manuscripts he also took over the idea that the originally pictographic nature of the Chinese written character was still a subsistent force, that the reader actually *saw* the image in the complex ideogram. All scholars now agree that this is mistaken; even if they did not, it is on the face of it impossible; as impossible as to suppose that the reader of English resuscitates every dead metaphor as he goes along, thinks of weighing when he ponders, or of the stars when he considers. Even though it was untrue, this way of thinking might have given rise, when applied to an Indo-European language, to some sort of doctrine of radical metaphor—that poetry proceeds by distilling the quintessence of language. This, we have been told, is one of the keys to Mallarmé. But Pound shows no interest in this sort of speculation. His supposed nugget of wisdom from the East is used to provide a cultural foundation for the doctrine of the image. Chinese uses picture writing and so ought we. A strain of crotchety hostility to the traditions of Western thinking begins to appear. An obscure ideological war is invented in which Confucius knocks out Aristotle, and abstraction and discursive thought are left in ruins. Poetry proceeds by the juxtaposition of ideograms, and new ideogram is old image writ large. The unit of poetry is the pictograph, the record of a significant glimpse. . . .

One of the most celebrated offshoots of the Imagist idea is Mr. Eliot's Objective Correlative. We are all heartily sick of the phrase, even Mr. Eliot, so I will only recall briefly its original formulation. "The only way of expressing emotion in the form of art is by finding an 'objective correlative'; in other words, a set of objects, a situation, a chain of events which shall be the formula of that *particular* emotion; such that when the external facts, which must terminate in sensory experience, are given, the emotion is immediately evoked." Objections have been made to the "expressionist" character of this passage—the suggestion that the business of the poet is to find external manifestations for previously determinate emotions. I wish to point to something rather different—the suggestion that the whole natural world offers to the poet a collection of bric-à-brac from which he takes selections to represent emotional states. "Direct presentation of the thing"—the image so produced exists to be one side of an equation the other side of which is an emotion. Plainly an eccentric view of the poet's procedure. We can hardly suppose that either the author of the *Iliad* or the author of

> Christ, that my love was in my arms
> And I in my bed again

were collecting *objets trouvés* in this way. Gerard Manley Hopkins wrote "The Wreck of the Deutschland" because he was moved by the account of a shipwreck in which five nuns were drowned; he did not go round looking for a suitable disaster to match an emotion that he already had. This is possibly a position that Mr. Eliot, who wrote of it a long time ago, would not wish to maintain in its full rigour. But we must in some sense hold him to it, for it has consequences in other parts of his thinking about poetry. There is the idea that coherence and validity of thought have nothing to do with poetic worth; Dante made great poetry out of a strong and beautiful philosophy, Shakespeare out of a muddled one, but this does not affect their merit as poets. There is the related idea that poets do not "think," they take over the thought of their time. This would make the poet's activity something like painting flowers on china plates that he had bought ready-made from the factory; and I am sure that this is not what Mr. Eliot means; but it is what he appears to be saying. There is the idea that meaning is a kind of sop thrown to the intellect, like the bit of meat the burglar keeps to give to the dog, while the "poetry" does its work. These are all pervasive ideas in modern, postsymbolist poetic strategy, and they are all related to the root idea that the substance of poetry is the image and its resonances.

The doctrine has its corollary when we come to consider the major structure of poetry; one that is startlingly at variance with the classical view. If poetry is a matching up of images with emotions its underlying framework consists of emotions. Its order is therefore an order of emotions. In classical poetic theory (by classical I mean here one that prevailed generally from the Greeks till some time in the nineteenth century) the order of poetry was an order of events or thoughts. Events are capable of casual connection, thoughts of logical connection; the one is the structure of narrative or dramatic poetry, the other of philosophic or reflective poetry. Only in the briefest lyric can we find an order that is simply that of emotions; and classical poetic theory was not deduced from brief lyrics. One does not insist on an Aristotelian rigour of construction; but even in the looser forms the sense of a syntax of events or a syntax of thoughts is preserved; and criticism insisted on it. Emotions are not capable of such a syntax. A pattern can be made of them, by simple juxtaposition, but it will hardly be an integrated pattern, unless there runs through it the thread of narrative or logic. Imagist poetry has therefore been obliged to invoke *another kind of logic*, a logic of emotions that works in its own way, and is supposed to be especially suitable for poetry. The most compendious expression of this notion is to be found in Mr. Eliot's introduction to St. John Perse's *Anabase*:

> any obscurity of the poem, on first readings, is due to the suppression of 'links in the chain,' of explanatory and connecting matter, and not to incoherence, or to the love of cryptogram. The justification of such abbreviation of method is that the sequence of images coincides and concentrates into one intense impression of barbaric civilisation. The reader has to allow the images to fall into his memory successively without questioning the reasonableness of each at the moment; so that, at the end, a total effect is produced.
>
> Such selection of a sequence of images and ideas has nothing chaotic about it. There is a logic of the imagination as well as a logic of concepts. People who do not appreciate poetry always find it difficult to distinguish between order and chaos in the arrangement of images; and even those who are capable of appreciating poetry cannot depend upon first impressions. I was not convinced of Mr. Perse's imaginative order until I had read the poem five or six times. And if, as I suggest, such an arrangement of imagery requires just as much 'fundamental brainwork' as the arrangement of an argument, it is to be expected that the reader of a poem should take at least as much trouble as a barrister reading an important decision on a complicated case.

This document is worth examining in some detail. The occasion is particular, but the application is general. What is outlined is the method of a school. Three layers are to be discerned in this ingenious piece of discourse. The first is simply descriptive. We are told of a "sequence of images," of images that fall into the memory successively with no question of reasonableness, of resultant obscurity. This is a general description of Imagist technique; it is the procedure of *Anabase*; it is also the procedure of *The Waste Land* and the *Cantos*. The second layer, interwoven with the first—but we are attempting to separate it—is one of justification. Two justifications of this method are in fact offered. They are not compatible with each other. The first is that any appearance of obscurity is merely due to the suppression of connecting matter: the logic of the poem is like the logic of any other kind of discourse, but it is presented in a concentrated and elliptical form. The second justification, however, is that the poem is constructed according to a "logic of the imagination" which is different from ordinary logic. It requires as much effort as the construction of an argument, but it is evidently of a different kind. And besides these layers, of description and justification, there is a third layer of knock-me-down *argumentum ad hominem*, designed to cause alarm and despondency in the breasts of persons who have not yet accepted the first two. Such persons do not appreciate poetry, cannot distinguish between order and chaos, and, in their benighted triviality, have probably never thought of assimilating the action of a reader of poetry to that of a barrister getting up a brief.

There is much in this sort of argument that arouses suspicion. The device of dismissing one's opponents as unqualified instead of convincing them that they are wrong is one that works only with the very unsophisticated or the very easily scared. It has been greatly overworked by the founding fathers of modern poetics. Only poets can judge poetry; this is a matter for the expert; certificates of culture countersigned by Confucius, Lancelot Andrewes and Rémy de Gourmont to be produced on admission—but these minatory gestures have dwindled into a curious historic ritual; and they have been discussed elsewhere. A more serious question is whether the Imagist procedure here described in an ordinary mode of discourse telescoped and abbreviated, or whether some special "logic of the imagination" is involved.

Let us look at the organisation of *The Waste Land*. In detail, and in some places, the first explanation works well enough. The twenty opening lines of the poem can be seen as an elliptical narrative, with fragments of reflection and direct speech. ("April is the cruellest month.... [we] went on in sunlight, into the Hofgarten.... And when we were children, staying at the archduke's.") In principle it could be expanded, the links could be supplied; what we have is the natural result of the attempt at pruning and concentrating nineteenth-century poetic method. The sense of an existing but not definitely stated plot is still there. It will require a great deal more latitude to apply this argument to the major structure of the poem. We know

now that it was of considerably greater length, and attained its present proportions under the direction of Ezra Pound. We have always known that "Death by Water," the Phlebas the Phoenician section, was not originally part of *The Waste Land*, since it is a translation from the French of the last section of an earlier poem "Dans le Restaurant." Its insertion was again due to Pound. We know too that "Gerontion" was at one time to be included but was in the end left out to become a separate poem. If this is the logic of the imagination it is evidently patient of a good deal of outside influence. There is a curious fortuitousness about it. And mere ellipsis, the omission of connecting links, will not serve as an explanation of the changes of speaker, shifts in time, scene and mode of address, the liberation of the image from all continuity that give the poem its peculiarly coruscating surface. In the poem as a whole the sense of an unspoken underlying plot has completely disappeared.

I cannot think that the problems raised by the structure of *The Waste Land* have been faced. They have been a party matter, a matter for polemic or defence; they have been a shibboleth; to accept this sort of technique was at one time a sort of touchstone for participation in modern poetry. Above all, the methodological anfractuosities of the piece have fulfilled one of the main economic functions of poetry in this century—they have given employment to a host of scholiasts. But they have hardly been a matter for disinterested enquiry. While the poem was still capable of causing bewilderment it established itself. The brilliance of the imagery, the auditory and incantatory grandeur of its best passages, stole into the consciousness and became a part of our poetical property; it became ungrateful, almost indecent to ask of what sort of continuum these fragments were a part. And we became satisfied with a level of coherence that we should never have found sufficient in any earlier poem. The unity of emotional effect withdrew attention from the logical discontinuity, the extraordinary rhetorical diversity. A poem about frustration, aridity, fear and the perversions of love—these signs were to be read by anyone. They were read, and in combination with the modern urban imagery they instigated the critics who said that the poem expressed "the disillusionment of a generation." For this, some years later, they were sternly reproved by the author; but they were no doubt expressing, in their way, the only sense they had of a unity of purpose in the poem. Meanwhile, prompted by the notes, many persons who had stopped reading *The Golden Bough* looked at it

again, and those who had never heard of Miss Jessie Weston read
From Ritual to Romance. None of them were bold enough to say in
public that these studies did little to advance their understanding.
Certainly they directed attention to recurring symbolism of death
and rebirth, drought and rain. But this was the kind of pattern that
in earlier poetry had been only secondary to structure of another
kind; it could not be seen as constituting a structure in itself. So we
turned to more peripheral matters. We looked up the quotations
from Dante and Baudelaire, and our apprehension of isolated lines
increased in depth. *Turdus aonalaschkae pallasii*, whose water-dripping
song is justly celebrated, doubtless afforded satisfaction to many.
And the volume of exegesis increased, the explanations that did not
explain, the links that connected nothing to nothing. And by the
time that the movement of modern poetry had gone far enough for
it to be a possible object of contemplation and enquiry, one shrank
from asking the real questions, lest what was after all one of the great
poetic experiences of our time should be still further buried beneath
yet another load of waste paper.

But the questions remain—above all the question of what really
makes the poem a totality, if it is one at all. If we can imagine some
ideal critic, acquainted with the poetical tradition of Europe, yet
innocent of the spirit of our age, and if we can imagine ourselves
persuading him to leave the question of total structure in abeyance,
"to allow the images to fall into his memory successively without
questioning the reasonableness of each"—he would still be struck by
the extraordinary rhetorical incongruities. He would find within its
four hundred lines passages that are narrative, others that are dramatic, descriptive, lyric, hallucinatory and allusive. The theory of
genres was never watertight or exhaustive, but never before was
there a poem of this length, or perhaps of any other length, in which
the modes were so mixed. Nor is the rhetorical level any more
constant than the rhetorical mode. A modern and highly individual
elegiac intensity, pastiche Renaissance grandeur, sharp antithetical
social comment in the Augustan manner, the low mimetic of public
house conversation—all these and probably several other styles are
found side by side. The relation of these is sometimes obvious; it is
one of calculated contrast. But it is a question how hard such contrasts of texture can be worked in a relatively short poem without
disastrous damage to the unity of surface. It is not so much in the
obvious collisions of the high and the low styles that this is felt. That

kind of calculated shock action is a limited effect, and the intention of producing the shock itself provides a medium between the two elements. It is the use of language in different and unrelated fashions in different parts of the poem that is disruptive. There is the lovely, romantically evocative manner of the hyacinth girl passage:

> Yet when we came back, late, from the Hyacinth
> garden,
> Your arms full, and your hair wet, I could not
> Speak, and my eyes failed, I was neither
> Living nor dead, and I knew nothing,
> Looking into the heart of light, the silence.

These lines live unhappily in the same poem with:

> Endeavours to engage her in caresses
> Which still are unreproved, if undesired.
> Flushed and decided, he assaults at once;
> Exploring hands encounter no defence;
> His vanity requires no response,
> And makes a welcome of indifference.

The uneasiness does not arise from incompatibility of tone and feeling but because the two passages are using language in utterly different ways; the first to evoke, by overtones and connotations, the trembling ghost of an intense emotion that is never located or defined; the second to define a situation by precise denotation and intelligent analysis. It is as though a painter were to employ a pointilliste technique in one part of a picture, and the glazes of the high renaissance in another.

When we come to the content of the separate passages the situation is disturbing in another way. It has become fashionable to refer to these contents as "themes," suggesting a vaguely musical analogy; and suggesting, too, I suppose, that the "themes" of a poem are related to each other only as the themes of a musical composition are. But themes in a poem are made of words, and words have meanings; our attention is never arrested at the verbal surface; it proceeds to what the words denote. They denote objects, persons and ideas; and it is very difficult altogether to dispel the notion that the objects, persons and ideas in a single poem should be in some intelligible relation to one another. A very little inspection of the commentaries, or questioning of readers of the poem, will show that this is not the case with *The Waste Land*; there is no certainty either about what is denoted, or how it is related to other denotations. It is sometimes suggested, for example, that the hyacinth girl is or might be the same as the lady who stayed with her cousin the archduke a few lines earlier. To me it has always been obvious that these fragmentary glimpses showed us, and were designed to show us, two different kinds of women and two different kinds of human relationship. I suppose that those who think otherwise have taken at least as much trouble and are no greater fools than I. And I see no means by which the matter could be decided.

We have already remarked that Phlebas the Phoenician had a prior existence in another context and was included by chance or outside suggestion. True, a place is rather arbitrarily prepared for him; Madame Sosostris the clairvoyant, who is supposed to be using a Tarot pack, produces the card of the drowned Phoenician sailor—which is not a member of the Tarot pack—in order to suggest in advance that Phlebas has some part in the structure of the poem. But what his part is remains quite uncertain. Here the commentators for the most part insist on resolutely marking time, for fear of committing themselves to a false step; and we are even bidden to observe that the "currents" which pick the drowned Phlebas's bones have a forerunner in the "currants" in the pocket of Mr. Eugenides the Smyrna merchant. Surely the last refuge of baffled imbecility.

It has been said that the poem adopts a "stream of consciousness" technique; and this sounds reassuring without committing us to anything very much. But it is precisely what the poem does not do. The advantage of the "stream of consciousness" technique is that it allows a flood of images, more or less emancipated from narrative or logical continuity, while still preserving a psychological continuity—the continuity of inhering in a single consciousness. *The Waste Land* conspicuously forgoes this kind of unifying principle. One desperate expedient has been to fasten on Mr. Eliot's note to line 218: "Tiresais, although a mere spectator and not indeed a 'character,' is yet the most important personage in the poem, uniting all the rest. . . . What Tiresias *sees*, in fact, is the substance of the poem." In the light of this it can be suggested that the whole poem is Tiresias's "stream of consciousness." This is probably to give the note more weight than it can bear, and in any case, it does little to the purpose. Who was Tiresias? A man who had also been a woman, who lived forever and

could foretell the future. That is to say, not a single human consciousness, but a mythological catchall, and as a unifying factor of
no effect whatever.

I should like to commit myself to the view that for a poem to
exist as a unity more than merely bibliographical, we need the sense
of one voice speaking, as in lyric or elegiac verse; or of several voices
intelligibly related to each other, as in narrative with dialogue or
drama; that what these voices say needs a principle of connection no
different from that which would be acceptable in any other kind of
discourse; that the collocation of images is not a method at all but
the negation of method. In fact, to expose oneself completely, I want
to say that a poem, internally considered, ought to make the same
kind of sense any other discourse.

This should amount to a frontal attack on the main positions of
modern poetics. I cannot feel that I have the equipment for this
enterprise, nor if I had that it would be the right way to proceed. If
the conviction I have baldly stated is just, its justice will be seen, in
due time not by virtue of a puny attack from a single criticaster, but
by what Johnson calls the common sense of readers uncorrupted by
literary prejudice. So I only wish to press my point in two directions
of which I feel fairly certain, neither of them quite central.

For the first I return to the sentence of Johnson I have just quoted.
"By the common sense of readers uncorrupted with literary preju-
dices, after all the refinements of subtlety and the dogmatism of
learning, must be finally decided all claim to poetical honours."
These are words that no one who cares about poetry in our century
can read without a twinge. The appeal to a body of readers who are
not specialists or eccentrics, who are merely representative of the
common sentiment and intelligence of human kind, is one we feel
ourselves so little able to make, one that we know so well, if we are
honest, ought to be made—that we can think of it only with a feeling
of distress. Where is contemporary poetry read, and where is it
written? In the universities. Who reads it? Students; professional
students of literature mostly, and professors, who expect to write
papers on it, or to lecture on it—to "explicate" it, in the current
technical cant. What has become (not to go back to some prelapsarian
Eden) of the kind of public that even so recent a poet as Tennyson
could enjoy? It has been warned off; it has been treated to sneers,
threats and enigmas. It has been told so often that it has no status
and no business in the sacred wood, and it has found the business

actually being transacted there so remote from its ordinary apprehension, that it has turned away, in indifference, or disgust, or despair. A complex of social reasons is often produced to account for
this; no doubt some of them are valid. A covert notion of social
determinism is invoked to produce a sensation of comforting hope-
lessness about almost any undesirable situation today. But that is not
my business. I am only concerned with what is intrinsic to poetry;
and much of the reason for the narrow appeal of modern poetry is
in the poetry itself. The wilful Alexandrianism, the allusiveness and
multiplicity of reference, above all, the deliberate cultivation of
modes of organisation that are utterly at variance with those of ordinary discourse—these are the main reasons for the disappearance
of Johnson's common reader. It is hard to say this, for to say it lines
one up with the hostile, the malicious and the Philistine, with all
those who hate and suspect the exploring sensibility and have never
made the attempt to penetrate into the imaginative life of their time.
But it is sometimes necessary to risk being put in bad company for
the sake of saying what seems to be true. One can only hope that
one has better reasons for saying it.

For my second point I hope to produce a better reason. The
poem that abandons the syntax of narrative or argument and relies
on the interplay of "themes" or the juxtaposition of images according
to the mysterious laws of poetic logic is not, so far as it is doing
anything positive at all, doing anything that poetry has not done
before. Clustered and repeated images, contrasts or echoes among
them, a half-heard music of this kind has always been part of poetic
effect. We have always partly known it, and modern criticism has
done much to make it explicit. But in all poetry before our time this
music has been background music. What we have heard with the
alert and directed attention has been something different. It has been
a story, or an argument, or a meditation, or the direct expression of
feeling. Modern criticism has aroused our sense of this second sub-
rational layer in our appreciation of poetry. Perhaps the most signal
instance of this is the Shakespeare criticism of Wilson Knight, which
sees the plays not as patterns made by character in action, but as
"expanded metaphors," patterns of "themes" and "images." Modern poetry in the Imagist mode has peformed the extraordinary man-
oeuvre of shifting its whole weight to this second level. It has shorn
itself of paraphrasable sense, of all narrative or discursive line, and
relies on the play of contrasted images alone. In doing so it has

achieved a startling concentration and brilliance of the individual image, and a whole new rhetoric of its own, with its own special kind of fascination. I still wish to maintain that it is an inadequate rhetoric, inadequate for anything but very short poems and very special effects—states of madness and dream, for example. I take it that the case of Pound's *Cantos* goes without saying; they are the wreckage of poetry; brilliant passages, sometimes long, sometimes the merest splinters, floating in a turbid sea of stammering and incoherent mumble. But even in *The Waste Land* and the *Four Quartets*, where the level of the individual passages is far more consistent, and where it is just possible to give their arrangement some sort of publicly valid justification, the organising principle is still quite inadequate for poems of this scope. These poems survive, and will survive not assisted by their structure but in spite of it.

This is true of much of the work of Pound, Eliot and Wallace Stevens—to name three of the founding fathers of modern poetry. Their poetry suffers, even on the level on which it functions so persuasively and brilliantly, from the lack of any other level, the lack of public, explicit, paraphrasable discourse. We know, of course, about the "heresy of paraphrase" as it has been called—that we ought never to suppose that a paraphrase can tell us what a poem is "about." Perhaps we ought never to paraphrase a poem; but as with many other things that we ought never to do, we ought also to be able to feel that we could do it. The virtue that we exercise in not making a conceptual prose translation of a modern poem is generally a fugitive and cloistered virtue; for it would not be possible to give any such translation if we tried. To attempt to explain to an intelligent person who knows nothing about twentieth-century poetry how *The Waste Land* works is to be overcome with embarrassment at having to justify principles so affected, so perverse, so deliberately removed from the ordinary modes of rational communication. If poetry were to go on in this way it would develop before long into an esoteric entertainment with as much relevance to the experience of the common reader as, say, heraldry or real tennis. The imagist revolution was a sort of spring-cleaning; a much-needed spring-cleaning that got rid of a great deal of the fusty, obstructive and dust-gathering matter that had cluttered up the weaker poetry of the nineteenth century. But the house has not been comfortable to live in ever since. And the clotted rubbish of academic imagist criticism is already beginning to fill it up again. There is no reason to be optimistic about this situation. Poetry can degenerate into a meaningless esoteric exercise, and go on that way for centuries. It has happened. But perhaps it will not happen to us. And we have the example of the greatest poet of the early twentieth century to show that it need not. It is something of a paradox that Yeats, whose beliefs are often supposed to be more fantastic and irrational than those of any other great mind of our time, should never have lost his faith in rational order and the disposing intelligence as the guiding principle of a poem.

The First *Waste Land*

Richard Ellmann

Lloyds' most famous bank clerk revalued the poetic currency fifty years ago. As Joyce said, *The Waste Land* ended the idea of poetry for ladies. Whether admired or detested, it became, like *Lyrical Ballads* in 1798, a traffic signal. Hart Crane's letters, for instance, testify to his prompt recognition that from that time forward his work must be to outflank Eliot's poem. Today footnotes do their worst to transform innovations into inevitabilities. After a thousand explanations, *The Waste Land* is no longer a puzzle poem, except for the puzzle of choosing among the various solutions. To be penetrable is not, however, to be predictable. The sweep and strangeness with which Eliot delineated despair resist temptations to patronize Old Possum as old hat. Particular discontinuities continue to surprise even if the idea of discontinuous form—to which Eliot never quite subscribed and which he was to forsake—is now almost as familiar as its sober counterpart. The compound of regular verse and *vers libre* still wears some of the effrontery with which in 1922 it flouted both schools. The poem retains the air of a splendid feat.

Eliot himself was inclined to poohpooh its grandeur. His chiseled comment, which F. O. Matthiessen quotes, disclaimed any intention of expressing "the disillusionment of a generation," and said that he did not like the word "generation" or have a plan to endorse anyone's "illusion of disillusion." To Theodore Spencer he remarked in hum-

From *Eliot in His Time*. © 1971 by Richard Ellmann. Princeton University Press, 1973.

bler mood, "Various critics have done me the honour to interpret the poem in terms of criticism of the contemporary world, have considered it, indeed, as an important bit of social criticism. To me it was only the relief of a personal and wholly insignificant grouse against life. It is just a piece of rhythmical grumbling."

This statement is prominently displayed by Mrs. Valerie Eliot in her excellent decipherment and elucidation of *The Waste Land* manuscript. If it is more than an expression of her husband's genuine modesty, it appears to imply that he considered his own poem, as he considered *Hamlet*, an inadequate projection of its author's tangled emotions, a Potemkin village rather than a proper objective correlative. Yet no one will wish away the entire civilizations and cities, wars, hordes of people, religions of East and West, and exhibits from many literatures in many languages that lined the Thames in Eliot's ode to dejection. And even if London was only his state of mind at the time, the picture he paints of it is convincing. His remark to Spencer, made after a lapse of years, perhaps catches up another regret, that the poem emphasized his *Groll* at the expense of much else in his nature. It identified him with a sustained severity of tone, with pulpited (though brief) citations of biblical and Sophoclean anguish, so that he became an Ezekiel or at least a Tiresias. (In the original version John the Divine made a Christian third among the prophets.) While Eliot did not wish to be considered merely a satirist in his earlier verse, he did not welcome either the public assumption that his poetic mantle had become a hairshirt.

In its early version *The Waste Land* was woven out of more kinds of material, and was therefore less grave and less organized. The first two sections had an overall title (each had its own title as well), "He Do the Police in Different Voices," a quotation from *Our Mutual Friend*. Dickens has the widow Higden say to her adopted child, "Sloppy is a beautiful reader of a newspaper. He do the Police in different voices." Among the many voices in the first version, Eliot placed at the very beginning a long, conversational passage describing an evening on the town, starting at "Tom's place" (a rather arch use of his own name), moving on to a brothel, and concluding with a bathetic sunrise:

> First we had a couple of feelers down at Tom's place,
> There was old Tom, boiled to the eyes, blind . . .
> —("I turned up an hour later down at Myrtle's place.

What d'y' mean, she says, at two o'clock in the morning,
I'm not in business here for guys like you;
We've only had a raid last week, I've been warned
    twice . . .
So I got out to see the sunrise, and walked home.

This vapid prologue Eliot decided, apparently on his own, to expunge, and went straight into the now familiar beginning of the
poem.

Other voices were expunged by Eliot's friend Ezra Pound, who
called himself the "sage homme" (male midwife) of the poem. Pound
had already published in 1920 his own elegy on a shipwrecked man,
Hugh Selwyn Mauberley. Except in the title, the hero is unnamed,
and like Eliot's protagonist, he is more an observing consciousness
than a person, as he moves through salons, esthetic movements, dark
thoughts of wartime deaths. But Mauberley's was an esthetic quest,
and Eliot deliberately omitted this from his poem in favor of a spiritual one. (He would combine the two later in *Four Quartets*.) When
Eliot was shown *Mauberley* in manuscript, he had remarked that the
meaning of a section in Part II was not so clear as it might be, and
Pound revised it accordingly.

Pound's criticism of *The Waste Land* was not of its meaning; he
liked its despair and was indulgent of its neo-Christian hope. He
dealt instead with its stylistic adequacy and freshness. For example,
there was an extended, unsuccessful imitation of *The Rape of the Lock*
at the beginning of "The Fire Sermon." It described the lady Fresca
(imported to the waste land from "Gerontion" and one day to be
exported to the States for the soft drink trade). Instead of making
her toilet like Pope's Belinda, Fresca is going to it, like Joyce's Bloom.
Pound warned Eliot that since Pope had done the couplets better,
and Joyce the defecation, there was no point in another round. To
this shrewd advice we are indebted for the disappearance of such
lines as:

    The white-armed Fresca blinks, and yawns, and gapes,
    Aroused from dreams of love and pleasant rapes.
    Electric summons of the busy bell
    Brings brisk Amanda to destroy the spell . . .
    Leaving the bubbling beverage to cool,
    Fresca slips softly to the needful stool,
    Where the pathetic tale of Richardson

> Eases her labour till the deed is done . . .
> This ended, to the steaming bath she moves,
> Her tresses fanned by little flutt'ring Loves;
> Odours, confected by the cunning French,
> Disguise the good old hearty female stench.

The episode of the typist was originally much longer and more laborious:

> A bright kimono wraps her as she sprawls
> In nerveless torpor on the window seat;
> A touch of art is given by the false
> Japanese print, purchased in Oxford Street.

Pound found the décor difficult to believe: "Not in that lodging house?" The stanza was removed. When he read the later stanza,

> —Bestows one final patronising kiss,
> And gropes his way, finding the stairs unlit;
> And at the corner where the stable is,
> Delays only to urinate, and spit,

he warned that the last two lines were "probably over the mark," and Eliot acquiesced by cancelling them.

Pound persuaded Eliot also to omit a number of poems that were for a time intended to be placed between the poem's sections, then at the end of it. One was a renewed thrust at poor Bleistein, drowned now but still haplessly Jewish and luxurious underwater:

> Full fathom five your Bleistein lies
> Under the flatfish and the squids.
>
> Graves' Disease in a dead jew's/man's eyes!
> Where the crab have eat the lids . . .
>
> That is lace that was his nose . . .
>
> Roll him gently side to side,
> See the lips unfold unfold
>
> From the teeth, gold in gold.

Pound urged that this, and several other mortuary poems, did not add anything, either to *The Waste Land* or to Eliot's previous work.

He had already written "the longest poem in the English langwidge. Don't try to bust all records by prolonging it three pages further." As a result of this resmithying by *il miglior fabbro*, the poem gained immensely in concentration. Yet Eliot, feeling too solemnized by it, thought of prefixing some humorous doggerel by Pound about its composition. Later, in a more resolute effort to escape the limits set by *The Waste Land*, he wrote *Fragment of an Agon*, and eventually, "somewhere the other side of despair," turned to drama.

Eliot's remark to Spencer calls *The Waste Land* a personal poem. His critical theory was that the artist should seek impersonality, but this was probably intended not so much as a nostrum as an antidote, a means to direct emotion rather than let it spill. His letters indicate that he regarded his poems as consequent upon his experiences. When a woman in Dublin (Mrs. Josephine MacNeill, from whom I heard the account) remarked that Yeats had never really felt anything, Eliot asked in consternation, "How can you say that?" *The Waste Land* compiled many of the nightmarish feelings he had suffered during the seven years from 1914 to 1921, that is, from his coming to England until his temporary collapse.

Thanks to the letters quoted in Mrs. Valerie Eliot's introduction, and to various biographical leaks, the incidents of these years begin to take shape. In 1914 Eliot, then on a travelling fellowship from Harvard, went to study for the summer at Marburg. The outbreak of war obliged him to make his way, in a less leisurely fashion than he had intended, to Oxford. There he worked at his doctoral dissertation on F. H. Bradley's *Appearance and Reality*. The year 1914–1915 proved to be pivotal. He came to three interrelated decisions. The first was to give up the appearance of the philosopher for the reality of the poet, though he equivocated about this by continuing to write reviews for philosophical journals for some time thereafter. The second was to marry, and the third to remain in England. He was helped to all three decisions by Ezra Pound, whom he met in September 1914. Pound had come to England in 1908 and was convinced (though he changed his mind later) that this was the country most congenial to the literary life. He encouraged Eliot to marry and settle, and he read the poems that no one had been willing to publish and pronounced his verdict, that Eliot "has actually trained himself *and* modernized himself *on his own*." Harriet Monroe, the editor of *Poetry*, must publish them, beginning with "The Love Song of J. Alfred Prufrock." It took Pound some time to bring her to the same view, and it was not until June 1915 that Eliot's first publication took place. This was also the month of his first marriage, on June 26. His wife was Vivien Haigh-Wood, and Eliot remained, like Merlin with another Vivian, under her spell, beset and possessed by her intricacies for fifteen years and more.

What the newlyweds were like is recorded by Bertrand Russell, whom Eliot had known at Harvard. In a letter of July 1915, which he quotes in his *Autobiography*, Russell wrote of dining with them: "I expected her to be terrible, from his mysteriousness; but she was not so bad. She is light, a little vulgar, adventurous, full of life—an artist I think he said, but I should have thought her an actress. He is exquisite and listless; she says she married him to stimulate him, but finds she can't do it. Obviously he married in order to be stimulated. I think she will soon be tired of him. He is ashamed of his marriage, and very grateful if one is kind to her." Vivien was to dabble in painting, fiction, and verse, her mobile aspirations an aspect of her increasing instability.

Eliot's parents did not take well to their son's doings, though they did not, as has been said by Robert Sencourt, cut him off. His father, president of the Hydraulic Press Brick Company of St. Louis, had expected his son to remain a philosopher, and his mother, though a poet herself, did not like the *vers libre* of "Prufrock" any better than the free and easy marriage. To both parents it seemed that bright hopes were being put aside for a vague profession in the company of a vague woman in a country only too distinctly at war. They asked to see the young couple, but Vivien Eliot was frightened by the perils of the crossing, perhaps also by those of the arrival. So Eliot, already feeling "a broken Coriolanus," as Prufrock felt a Hamlet *manqué*, took the ship alone in August for the momentous interview.

His parents urged him to return with his wife to a university career in the States. He refused: he would be a poet, and England provided a better atmosphere in which to write. They urged him not to give up his dissertation when it was so near completion, and to this he consented. He parted on good enough terms to request their financial help when he got back to London, and they sent money to him handsomely, as he acknowledged—not handsomely enough, however, to release him from the necessity of very hard work. He taught for a term at the High Wycombe Grammar School, between Oxford and London, and then for two terms at Highgate Junior School. He completed his dissertation and was booked to sail on

April 1, 1916, to take his oral examination at Harvard; when the crossing was cancelled, his academic gestures came to an end. In March 1917 he took the job with Lloyds Bank, in the Colonial and Foreign Department, at which he stuck for eight years.

During the early months of their marriage the Eliots were helped also by Russell, who gave them a room in his flat, an act of benevolence not without complications for all parties. Concerned for his wife's health, and fearful—it may be—that their sexual difficulties (perhaps involving psychic impotence on his part) might be a contributing factor, Eliot sent her off for a two-week holiday with Russell. The philosopher found the couple none the less devoted to each other but noted in Mrs. Eliot a sporadic impulse to be cruel towards her husband not with simple but with Dostoevskyan cruelty. "I am every day getting things more right between them," Russell boasted, "but I can't let them alone at present, and of course I myself get very much interested." the Dostoevskyan quality affected his imagery: "She is a person who lives on a knife-edge, and will end as a criminal or a saint—I don't know which yet. She has a perfect capacity for both."

The personal life out of which came Eliot's personal poem now began to be lived in earnest. Vivien Eliot suffered obscurely from nerves, her health was subject to frequent collapses, she complained of neuralgia, of insomnia. Her journal for January 1, 1919, records waking up with migraine, "the worst yet," and staying in bed all day without moving; on September 7, 1919, she records "bad pain in right side, very very nervous." Ezra Pound, who knew her well, was worried that the passage in *The Waste Land*,

> "My nerves are bad to-night. Yes, bad. Stay with me.
> Speak to me. Why do you never speak? Speak.
> What are you thinking of? What thinking? What?
> I never know what you are thinking. Think."

might be too photographic. But Vivien Eliot, who offered her own comments on her husband's verse (and volunteered two excellent lines for the lowlife dialogue in "A Game of Chess") marked the same passage as "Wonderful." She relished the presentation of her symptoms in broken metre. She was less keen, however, on another line from this section, "The ivory men make company between us," and got her husband to remove it. Presumably its implications were too close to the quick of their marital difficulties. The reference may have been to Russell, whose attentions to Vivien were intended to keep the two together. Years afterwards Eliot made a fair copy of *The Waste Land* in his own handwriting, and reinserted the line from memory. (It should now be added to the final text.) But he had implied his feelings six months after his marriage when he wrote in a letter to Conrad Aiken, "I have lived through material for a score of long poems in the last six months."

Russell commented less sympathetically about the Eliots later, "I was fond of them both, and endeavoured to help them in their troubles until I discovered that their troubles were what they enjoyed." Eliot was capable of estimating the situation shrewdly himself. In his poem "The Death of Saint Narcissus," which *Poetry* was to publish in 1917 and then, probably because he withdrew it as too close to the knuckle, failed to do so, and which he thought for a time of including in *The Waste Land*, Eliot wrote of his introspective saint, "his flesh was in love with the burning arrows. . . . As he embraced them his white skin surrendered itself to the redness of blood, and satisfied him." For Eliot, however, the search for suffering was not contemptible. He was remorseful about his own real or imagined feelings, he was self-sacrificing about hers, he thought that remorse and sacrifice, not to mention affection, has value. In the Grail legends which underlie *The Waste Land*, the Fisher King suffers a Dolorous Stroke that maims him sexually. In Eliot's case The Dolorous Stroke has been marriage. He was helped thereby to the poem's initial clash of images, "April is the cruellest month," as well as to hollow echoes of Spencer's *Prothalamion* ("Sweet Thames, run softly till I end my song"). From the barren winter of his academic labors Eliot had been roused to the barren springtime of his nerve-wracked marriage. His life spread into paradox.

Other events of these years seem reflected in the poem. The war, though scarcely mentioned, exerts pressure. In places the poem may be a covert memorial to Henry Ware Eliot, the unforgiving father of the ill-adventured son. Vivien Eliot's journal records on January 8, 1919, "Cable came saying Tom's father is dead. Had to wait all day till Tom came home and then to tell him. *Most terrible.*" Eliot's first explicit statement of his intention to write a long poem comes in letters written later in this year. The references to "the king my father's death" probably derive as much from this actual death as from *The Tempest*, to which Eliot's notes evasively refer. As for the drowning of the young sailor, whether he is Ferdinand or a

Phoenician, the war furnished Eliot with many examples, such as Jean Verdenal, a friend from his Sorbonne days, who was killed in the Dardanelles. (Verdenal has received the posthumous distinction of being called Eliot's lover, but in fact the rumors of homosexuality—not voiced directly in Sencourt's biography but whispered in all its corners—remain unwitnessed.) But the drowning may be as well an extrapolation of Eliot's feeling that he was now fatherless as well as rudderless. The fact that the principal speaker appears in a new guise in the last section, with its imagery of possible resurrection, suggests that the drowning is to be taken symbolically rather than literally, as the end of youth. Eliot was addicted to the portrayal of characters who had missed their chances, become old before they had really been young. So the drowned sailor, like the buried corpse, may be construed as the young Eliot, himself an experienced sailor, shipwrecked in or about *l'an trentièsme de son eage*, like the young Pound in the first part of *Hugh Selwyn Mauberley* or Mauberley himself later in that poem, memorialized only by an oar.

It has been thought that Eliot wrote *The Waste Land* in Switzerland while recovering from a breakdown. But much of it was written earlier, some in 1914 and some, if Conrad Aiken is to be believed, even before. A letter to John Quinn indicates that much of it was on paper in May 1921. The breakdown, or rather, the rest cure, did give Eliot enough time to fit the pieces together and add what was necessary. At the beginning of October 1921 he consulted a prominent neurologist, who advised three months away from remembering "the profit and loss" in Lloyds Bank. When the bank had agreed, Eliot went first to Margate and stayed for a month from October 11. There he reported with relief to Richard Aldington that his "nerves" came not from overwork but from an "aboulie" (Hamlet's and Prufrock's disease) "and emotional derangement which has been a lifelong affliction." But, whatever reassurance this diagnosis afforded, he resolved to consult Dr. Roger Vittoz, a psychiatrist in Lausanne. He rejoined Vivien and on November 18 went with her to Paris. It seems fairly certain that he discussed the poem at that time with Ezra Pound. In Lausanne, where he went by himself, Eliot worked on it and sent revisions to Pound and to Vivien. Some of the letters exchanged between him and Pound survive. By early January 1922 he was back in London, making final corrections. The poem was published in October.

The manuscript had its own history. In gratitude to John Quinn,

the New York lawyer and patron of the arts, Eliot presented it to him.
Quinn died in 1924, and most of his possessions were sold at auction;
some, however, including the manuscript, were inherited by his sister. When the sister died, her daughter put many of Quinn's papers in
storage. But in the early 1950's she searched among them and found
the manuscript, which she then sold to the Berg Collection of the
New York Public Library. The then curator enjoyed exercising seig-
norial rights over the collection, and kept secret the whereabouts of
the manuscript. After his death its existence was divulged, and Valerie Eliot was persuaded to do her knowledgeable edition.

   She did so the more readily, perhaps, because her husband had
always hoped that the manuscript would turn up as evidence of
Pound's critical genius. It is a classic document. No one will deny
that it is weaker throughout than the final version. Pound comes off
very well indeed; his importance is comparable to that of Louis
Bouilhet in the history of composition of *Madame Bovary*. Yeats,
who also sought and received Pound's help, described it to Lady
Gregory: "To talk over a poem with him is like getting you to put
a sentence into dialect. All becomes clear and natural." Pound could
not be intimidated by pomposity, even Baudelairean pomposity:

> London, the swarming life you kill and breed,
> Huddled between the concrete and the sky;
> Responsive to the momentary need,
> Vibrates unconsious to its formal destiny.

Next to this he wrote "B-11-S." (His comments appear in red ink
on the printed transcription that is furnished along with photographs
of the manuscript.) Pound was equally peremptory about a passage
that Eliot seems to have cherished, perhaps because of childhood
experiences in sailing. It was the depiction at the beginning of "Death
by Water" of a long voyage, a modernizing and americanizing of
Ulysses' final voyage as given by Dante, but joined with sailing
experiences of Eliot's youth:

> Kingfisher weather, with a light fair breeze,
> Full canvas, and the eight sails drawing well.
> We beat around the cape and laid our course
> From the Dry Salvages to the eastern banks.
> A porpoise snored upon the phosphorescent swell,

> A triton rang the final warning bell
> Astern, and the sea rolled, asleep.

From these lines Pound was willing to spare only

> with a light fair breeze
> We beat around the cape from the Dry Salvages.
> A porpoise snored on the swell.

All the rest was—seamanship and literature. It became clear that the whole passage might as well go, and Eliot asked humbly if he should delete Phlebas as well. But Pound was as eager to preserve the good as to expunge the bad: he insisted that Phlebas stay because of the earlier references to the drowned Phoenician sailor. With equal taste, he made almost no change in the last section of the poem, which Eliot always considered to be the best, perhaps because it led into his subsequent verse. It marked the resumption of almost continuous form.

Eliot did not bow to all his friend's revisions. Pound feared the references to London might sound like Blake, and objected specifically to the line,

> To where Saint Mary Woolnoth kept the time,
> With a dead sound on the final stroke of nine.

Eliot wisely retained them, only changing "time" to "hours." Next to the passage,

> "You gave my hyacinths first a year ago;
> "They called me the hyacinth girl,"

Pound marked "Marianne," and evidently feared—though Mrs. Eliot's note indicates that he has now forgotten and denies it—that the use of quotation marks would look like an imitation of Marianne Moore. (He had warned Miss Moore of the equivalent danger of sounding like Eliot in a letter of December 16, 1918.) But Eliot, for whom the moment in the Hyacinth garden had obsessional force—it was based on feelings, though not on a specific incident in his own life—made no change.

Essentially Pound could do for Eliot what Eliot could not do for himself. There was some reciprocity, not only in *Mauberley* but in the *Cantos*. When the first three of these appeared in *Poetry* in 1917, Eliot offered criticism which was followed by their being completely altered. It appears, from the revised versions, that he objected to the elaborate windup, and urged a more direct confrontation of the reader and the material. A similar theory is at work in Pound's changes in *The Waste Land*. Chiefly by excision, he enabled Eliot to tighten his form and get "an outline," as he wrote in a complimentary letter of January 24, 1922. The same letter berated himself for "always exuding my deformative secretions in my own stuff. . . ." and for "going into nacre and objets d'art." Yet if this was necessity for Pound, he soon resolved to make a virtue of it, and perhaps partially in reaction in Eliot's form, he studied out means of loosening his own in the *Cantos*. The fragments which Eliot wished to shore and reconstitute Pound was willing to keep unchanged, and instead of mending consciousness, he allowed it to remain "disjunct" and its experiences to remain "intermittent." Fits and starts, "spots and dots," seemed to Pound to render reality much more closely then the outline to which he helped his friend. He was later to feel that he had gone wrong, and made a botch instead of a work of art. Notwithstanding his doubts, the *Cantos*, with their violent upheaval of sequence and location, stand as a rival eminence to *The Waste Land* in modern verse.

The Waste Land and the *Descensus ad Inferos*

Bernard F. Dick

In myth and fairy tale, the descent to the underworld was the highest form of the supernatural, surpassing omens, dreams, and prodigies by compelling belief in a mortal who entered the infernal portals and returned alive to the upper world. Originally the *descensus ad inferos* arose from the desire "to gain information about the future, or what is 'ahead' in terms of the lower cycle of life" by taking a trip to the lower world itself; but as the descent made the transition from *Märchen*, where it only satisfied man's penchant for the irrational, to epic, where it afforded a loftier vision of reality, the knowledge of the future became, in literary terms, the knowledge of character and event. By Homer's time, the descent or *katabasis* was clearly a literary technique which, like other epic conventions, retained some of its ritual vestiges; it had ceased being merely an attempt to satisfy the audience's curiosity about the hereafter and instead had crystallized into a type of dramatic foreshadowing.

In classical epic, the two major *descensus ad inferos, Odyssey* XI and *Aeneid* VI, exhibit a common descent pattern which might be outlined as follows:

(1) The descent is initiated by someone prophetically endowed, either a seer or a shade, who addresses the hero in direct and exhortative language, ordering him to embark on a journey designed to give him knowledge of the future. This knowledge will have a

From *Canadian Review of Literature* 2, no. 1 (Winter 1975). © 1975 by the Canadian Comparative Literature Association.

twofold function: it will clarify the hero's fate and at the same time will determine events occuring later in the epic, in much the same way as the witches' prophecies in *Macbeth*, by their gradual fulfilment, create a microcosmic unity within the tragic macrocosm.

In the *Odyssey*, it is Circe who tells Odysseus he must sail across Ocean to meet Teiresias in the land of the dead (X, 505–40). As the daughter of Helios, Circe naturally possesses the foreknowledge Odysseus lacks. Therefore, she can speak to him in the language of the epic command (ὥς σε κελεύω). It is also clear that Odysseus must make his voyage to gain information: χρειώ με κατήγαγεν εἰς Ἀίδαο/ψυχῇ χρησόμενον Θηβαίου Τειρεσίαο· ["I came here, driven to the land of death/in want of prophecy from Teiresias' shade," tr. Fitzgerald] (XI, 164–65).

In the *Aeneid*, Anchises' shade appears to Aeneas, demanding a meeting in the underworld where his son will acquire knowledge of the nation he will found: "tum genus omne tuum et quae dentur moenia disces" ["Then you will hear of your whole race to come/and what walled town is given you," tr. Fitzgerald] (V, 737). His mystagogue will be the Cumaean Sibyl, who proposes three ritual imperatives (VI, 145–53)—plucking the golden bough ("carpe manu"), burying Misenus ("conde sepulchro"), and sacrificing black cattle ("duc nigras pecudes")—before the descent can begin.

The knowledge the initiate acquires foreshadows subsequent events in the epic. In the *Odyssey*, Elpenor's shade predicted that Odysseus would return to Aeaea (XI, 69–70): the prediction was fulfilled at the beginning of Book XII. The return to Circe's island was dramatically necessary, since Odysseus required further information about his *nostos*. This Circe provided by synopsizing his last three adventures—the Sirens, Scylla, and Charybdis, and the Oxen of the Sun—which occurred exactly in the order in which she foretold them. Teiresias prophesied Odysseus' return to Ithaca without his comrades and his vengeance on the suitors (XI, 110–18), both of which came to pass in Books XIII and XXII respectively.

Prior to Aeneas' descent, the Sibyl delivered an extended prophecy which was fulfilled in the later books of the *Aeneid*:

> bella, horrida bella
> et Thybrim multo spumantem sanguine cerno.
> non Simois tibi nec Xanthus nec Dorica castra
> defuerint; alius Latio iam partus Achilles,

natus et ipse dea; nec Teucris addita Iuno
usquam aberit, cum tu supplex in rebus egenis
quas gentes Italum aut quas non oraveris urbes!
causa mali tanti coniunx iterum hospita Teucris
externique iterum thalami.
tu ne cede malis, sed contra audentior ito,
quam tua te Fortuna sinet. via prima salutis,
quod minime reris, Graia pandetur ab urbe.

(VI, 86–97)

[Wars, vicious wars
I see ahead, and Tiber foaming blood.
Simoïs, Xanthus, Dorians encamped—
You'll have them all again, with an Achilles,
Child of Latium, he, too, goddess-born.
And nowhere from pursuit of Teucrians
Will Juno stray, while you do destitute,
Begging so many tribes and towns for aid.
The cause of suffering here again will be
A bride foreign to Teucrians, a marriage
Made with a stranger.
Never shrink from blows.
Boldly, more boldly where your luck allows,
Go forward, face them. A first way to safety
Will open where you reckon on it least,
From a Greek city. (tr. Fitzgerald)]

The wars are those that will be waged in Latium, whose rivers, the
Numicius and the Tiber, parallel the Xanthus and the Simois of Troy.
The second Achilles is Turnus, and the foreign bride Lavinia. The
urbs Graia that will come to Aeneas' aid is Pallanteum, which Evander
founded on the Palatine Hill.

(2) The foreknowledge of the woman who prepares the hero
for the descent is limited to the immediate future. Circe can instruct
Odysseus only in the general details of his voyage and in the ritual
sacrifices he must make, but it is Teiresias who holds the key to the
hero's future. It is Teiresias, not Circe, who prophesies Odysseus'
return (Book XIII), his revenge (Book XXII), and his death, which
does not occur in the *Odyssey* but in the *Telegony*, the last poem of
the *Epic Cycle*, of which the *Iliad* and the *Odyssey* are part. Likewise

the Sibyl knows of events that will happen in Latium, but she is unaware of the role Aeneas will play in the history of Rome; it is Anchises who informs Aeneas of his cosmic destiny. Within the mantic hierarchy, the prophetess (Circe, the Sibyl) yields to the prophet (Teiresias, Anchises); female yields to male.

(3) In Hades, the hero sees, encounters, or learns about (a) a close friend seeking burial (Elpenor in the *Odyssey*, Palinurus in the *Aeneid*); (b) war heroes; (c) mythological heroines ill-fated in love; (d) the damned.

(4) In both the Homeric and Vergilian underworlds there is an indifference to topography that would not be remedied until Dante. Strictly speaking, Odysseus does not make a *katabasis*; he merely digs a trench from which the dead arise at the smell of the blood from the sacrificed animals. But through Homer's subtle narrative art, one feels Odysseus is travelling through certain regions of the underworld while, in effect, the underworld has come to him. In the interpolated ending of Book XI, Odysseus beholds the house of Hades, Orion in the field of asphodel, Tityus lying on the ground, and Tantalus standing in a pool; yet he has not moved from the trench. Of course, no *katabasis* can withstand logical analysis, and one must conclude that Homer and his interpolator were not overly concerned about infernal topography.

Vergil's hell is somewhat more specific; first of all, it is a place ("domus"), with threshold ("limen") and doors ("fores") leading to an interior: "Vergil seems to conceive of Hades as an extensive region with a spacious courtyard; leading to the court is a narrow entrance way; beyond the court are doors leading into the main quarters, and ultimately to the palace of Pluto." [Henry W. Prescott, *The Development of Virgil's Art* (1927; rpt New York: Russell & Russell 1963).] However, Vergil does not provide a one-to-one ratio between a Roman house and the underworld. Hades consists of "inania regna," and while these "unsubstantial realms" comprise certain parts of regions, they can have only the barest suggestion of shape.

"Hinc via, Tartarei quae fert Acherontis ad undas" ["Hence a road leads to the waters of Tartarean Acheron," tr. Fairclough] (VI, 295). But from where does the road lead to Acheron? Presumably from the entrance court. Vergil's Hades, then, is a shell of a house irrigated by subterranean rivers; it is a house which one enters through a volcanic cave and leaves through the gate of false dreams. The Vergilian *lacrimae rerum* extend even to hell, enshrouding it with an oceanic sadness that makes its divisions as tenuous as human life itself.

(5) Time in the *descensus* is a fiction; the poet wishes to dispel human notions of chronology, a characteristic of a contingent universe, by having the hero see and experience what can never be seen and experienced in terms of measured motion. Yet at the same time the mimetic tradition requires that the descent be narrated within some kind of continuum to which the poet can adhere when he wishes to achieve verisimilitude or from which he can depart when he chooses to depict infinity. Thus Odysseus travels from Aeaea across Ocean to the Land of the Cimmerians and back again in literally epic time, which has no parallel in the real world. In the *Aeneid* (VI, 539), the Sibyl interrupts Aeneas' conversation with Deiphobus by reminding him that night is approaching and that they are wasting time ("ducimus horas"), although he is in a realm where the eternal has subsumed the temporal. However, he is also in the realm of literature where a descent, although set *sub specie aeternitatis*, must be accomplished "on time."

All of these characteristics of the *descensus* appear in *The Waste Land*. There is not, nor will there by, any one approach to Eliot's poem that is completely satisfying, and only the most humanistic scholars have studied it without growing to hate it. Its dualism (classical past vs sullied present, West vs East, orchestration vs structure) grows into a pluralism, its fragments into contexts, and their interpretations into rebuttals. *The Waste Land* is a theorem with an infinity of corollaries. However, if the poem is regarded as a descent to the underworld, many of its problems, particularly the unstable topography and the shifting chronology, can be resolved as conventions of the *descensus* where time and place are structural devices that make the spiritual intelligible in human terms. Some have claimed that *The Waste Land* is one day in a living hell—from morning to evening, from the "brown fog" to the "violet hour." This is as true as saying that *Aeneid* VI covers a period from dawn to shortly before midnight or that *The Divine Comedy* covers a period of seven days. It is equally true to say, as Eliot did later:

I can only say, *there* we have been: but I cannot say where.
And I cannot say, how long, for that is to place it in time.

["Burnt Norton," II]

It is a critical commonplace to regard Teiresias the androgyne as the poem's many-voiced speaker who, in remembering the past, becomes the past and those who formed it. Certainly one of Teiresias' clearest voices is that of a quester recalling his journey through hell in search of knowledge both personal and cosmic. In the earlier drafts of *The Waste Land*, there was a stage before Teiresias awoke from the lassitude of winter to the cruelty of spring; a stage before he was a suffering initiate making the rounds of hell with his Tarot card in lieu of a golden bough. Before Teiresias was a quester, he was a picaro, as one learns from the original manuscript, which opened with a surrealistic night on the town, reminiscent of the phantasmagoric wanderings of the young trio in Petronius' *Satyricon*.

In "He Do the Police in Different Voices" (I), we see Teiresias before he discovered April was the cruellest month; we also see why winter kept him warm. *The Waste Land* originally began with Teiresias remembering a winter evening in Boston when he was a dapper and carefree bachelor: some drinks, dinner, a show, an after-theatre gin at the Opera Exchange, an evening stroll where a friend gets lost and ends up in a brothel, a near-arrest, a Chaplinesque cab drive, and a walk home in the glow of sunrise.

Teiresias' first incarnation as a rogue was not terribly memorable, nor was the chatty vernacular of his first voice:

> First we had a couple of feelers at Tom's place,
> There was old Tom, boiled to the eyes, blind,
> (Don't you remember that time after a dance,
> Top hats and all, we and Silk Hat Harry,
> And old Tom took us behind, brought out a
>   bottle of fizz,
> With old Jane, Tom's wife; and we got Joe to sing
> "I'm pround of all the Irish blood that's in me,
> "There's not a man can say a word agin me").
>   ("He Do the Police in Different Voices," I, 1–8)

Teiresias is not yet a poet. However, between the time he walked home in the sunrise and the time he discovered that April was the cruellest month, he was transformed from an irresponsible gadabout to an introspective initiate and transferred from Boston to London. The logic of the transition is the logic of the dream, the same logic one finds in the *Satyricon* where the young men move like figures in an animated cartoon from a rhetoric class to a brothel, from an orgy to a banquet. One finds a similar logic in the cinema where a director can cut from one state of mind to another and can manipulate geography as if time and space had no objective significance. One will never know what happened to Teiresias en route, except that he underwent a change of voice from garrulous undergraduate to reflective *littérateur* and a change of personality from picaro to quester. He is now ready to play a role performed earlier by Gilgamesh, Odysseus, Aeneas, and Dante the pilgrim; but he requires guidance and thus visits Madame Sosostris, the archetypal female mystagogue; who, like Circe and the Sibyl, speaks to him in demonstrative and exhortative language:

> Here, said she,
> Is your card, the drowned Phoenician Sailor,
> (Those are pearls that were his eyes. Look!)
> Here is Belladonna, the Lady of the Rocks,
> The lady of situations.
> Here is the man with three staves, and here the
>   Wheel,
> And here is the one-eyed merchant, and this card,
> Which is blank, is something he carries on his back,
> Which I am forbidden to see. I do not find
> The Hanged Man. Fear death by water.
> I see crowds of people, walking around in a ring.
>   (lines 46–56)

Madame Sosostris' reading of the Tarot forms the microcosm of the poem. She gives Teiresias the card of the drowned Phoenician sailor whose fate is recorded in Part IV. Next comes Belladonna, the negative of the Tarot Empress who rules the barren and synthetic kingdom depicted in "A Game of Chess." In his notes, Eliot "quite arbitrarily" associates "the man with three staves" with the Fisher King into whom Teiresias merges in Part III. The "one-eyed merchant" is a variant of the Tarot fool who appears as Mr Eugenides, the Smyrna merchant, in Part III. There is no blank card in the Tarot; perhaps the clairvoyant does not know her trade as well as she should. The "Wheel" is the wheel of fortune on which the crowd revolves. "The Hanged Man" is missing from the deck; he is Christ who cannot inhabit a *terre gaste* and who appears in disguise as the hooded figure of Part V. "Fear death by water" is understandable advice from one who is ignorant of its salvific power; it will not be until Part IV that one realizes death by water can mean rebirth. "Crowds of people, walking round in a ring" are the crowds Teiresias sees crossing London Bridge. By her reading, Madame Sosostris has introduced the leading characters and major themes of *The Waste Land*, just as by her prophecy the Cumaean Sibyl provided a context for the last six books of the *Aeneid*.

After Teiresias receives his card, he begins his *descensus* into the hell of the living dead who make up in density what they lack in spiritual depth. Like Odysseus and Aeneas, he first sees the anonymous dead, not any specific shade:

> A crowd flowed over London Bridge, so many,
> I had not thought death had undone so many.
>
> (lines 62–63)

Eliot's shades throng London Bridge like the *umbrae* of the *Aeneid* pressing against the banks of the infernal river. Interestingly, both poets use the same image of the shades "flowing": Eliot's crowd over London Bridge, Vergil's crowd (VI, 305) to the banks of the Styx ("huc omnis turba ad ripas effusa ruebat" ["Here a whole crowd came flowing to the banks"]).

Next Teiresias encounters an individual *umbra* and addresses him with mock-heroic solemnity:

> There I saw one I knew, and stopped him, crying: "Stetson!
> You who were with me in the ships at Mylae!
> That corpse you planted last year in your garden,
> Has it begun to sprout? Will it bloom this year?"
>
> (lines 69–72)

Stetson served with Teiresias, however anachronistically, at Mylae; their meeting recalls the confrontation in the classical underworld between the initiate and a warrior shade—Odysseus with Agamemnon and Achilles, Aeneas with Deiphobus.

The classical underworld, like classical rhetoric, is founded on the principle of *gradatio*: a continuous movement from the less specific toward the more specific to the climactically specific. Thus Aeneas moves from a formless entrance court into a realm that grows more defined as he advances toward Elysium, the climax of his *descensus ad inferos*. So, too, does Teiresias move from the general "crowd" to those who compose it: Stetson, an old comrade-in-arms, and now

Belladonna, an old amour, whose rococo boudoir is a hell of history ignored and art misused.

Belladonna's room is a peculiar kind of hell: a hell of unheeded evocations of the past. One should recall the beginning of *Aeneid* VI which furnishes the necessary analogue. When Aeneas landed at Cumae, his fancy was struck by the sculptured doors of the temple of Apollo which Daedalus adorned with scenes from his bondage in Crete: the yearly tribute to the Minotaur, Pasiphaë and the bull, and the fall of Icarus which the artist's grief prevented his completing. In Vergil, art produces the *lacrimae rerum*; yet art can only produce this surge of cosmic sadness when the beholder understands the labour involved in forging fragments of personal experience into panels of history. Belladonna's room is haunted by the past; actually, the room is a classical iconograph complete with Dido's laquearia, a mural depicting the metamorphosis of Philomela, and "other withered stumps of time . . . told upon the walls" (lines 104–5).

Belladonna does not realize she is surrounded by antiquity; unlike Aeneas, she cannot view the past within a historical context since its meaning has evanesced like the smoke from her candles. The vision of art that was the prelude to Aeneas' descent has become a meaningless trapping of Belladonna's hell.

Throughout most of *The Waste Land*, hell is a city and thus allows for more diversity than either the trench Odysseus digs or the "inania regna" Aeneas traverses. Teiresias now finds himself in a new setting, a pub where Bill, Lou, and Mae listen to an anonymous woman (the speaker of the poem in a feminine mode) relate the story of Lil who spent her husband's army pay for an abortion instead of false teeth.

The narrator speaks like an *umbra*, someone totally oblivious to time ("HURRY UP PLEASE ITS TIME"). As a shade, she knows only the past (the abortion, the false teeth, the Sunday dinner to which she was asked) and the future (Albert's reaction to Lil's physical decline) but not the present. Significantly, the narrator and her story dissipate amid ghostly goodbyes.

In "The Fire Sermon," where time and geography intermingle like memory and desire, we find Teiresias in a different part of the city. Now a Fisher King, he sits on the banks of the Thames, anticipating a gathering of the shades. Like Odysseus, he does not move; instead, the dead come to him:

But at my back from time to time I hear
The sound of horns and motors, which shall bring
Sweeney to Mrs Porter in the spring.
O the moon shone bright on Mrs Porter
And on her daughter
They wash their feet in soda water
Et O ces voix d'enfants, chantant dans la coupole!

Twit twit twit
Jug jug jug jug jug jug
So rudely forc'd.
Tereu

Unreal City

(lines 196–207)

The entire sequence is a phantasmagoria. The horns and motors orchestrate a cacophonous prelude to the reunion of Sweeney and Mrs Porter, whose penchant for hygiene evokes the infamous ballad about her and her daughter. Teiresias' subconscious associates the ballad with the singing of the children in Verlaine's *Parsifal*, where their youthful voices arouse pederastic desires in the knight. The song of the children evokes the cry of the nightingale and the myth of Philomela's metamorphosis after her rape by Tereus, now a mere vocative ("Tereu") whose terminal -u, almost a ululation, propels the protagonist to the unreal city where Mr Eugenides is waiting with a pocket full of currants and an ambiguous invitation to luncheon and a weekend in Brighton.

As the wheel turns in accordance with Madame Sosostris' prediction, next to revolve on it are a typist and a pimply clerk. After witnessing their automated intercourse, Teiresias is transported from the typist's dingy flat to the Church of St Magnus the Martyr at the foot of London Bridge. Here one of the most familiar features of the *descensus* appears: the infernal river. In an extended lyrical passage that is almost a *Lied*, the Thames is described in two different periods of history: the modern age when it "sweats oil and tar" and the Age of Elizabeth when "the brisk swell / rippled both shores" (lines 284–85). The Thames that runs through the waste land is a river of woe, an Acheron, a Rhine plundered of its gold. The cry of the Rhine Maidens from *Die Götterdämmerung* ("Weialala leia") becomes the cry of the Thames Maidens who yearn for a past when the "gilded shell" of Elizabeth's barge graced their waters.

The Thames Maidens constitute another element of the *descensus*: the catalogue of women. In the classical underworld, the hero sees women from mythology who suffered for love. Odysseus beheld Tyro, Alcmena, Megara, Jocasta, Chloris, Leda, Phaedra, Procris, and Ariadne among others. In the *Lugentes Campi*, Aeneas saw Phaedra, Procris, Eriphyle, Evadne, Pasiphaë, Laodamia, and last of all, Dido. The Thames Maidens were also badly used in the game of love; one was seduced in the borough of Richmond, another in Moorgate, the third at Margate. However, none of them has the grandeur of a Phaedra, a Dido, or even a Procris. They are little more than prostitutes lamenting their betrayal and lost virginity.

The Thames Maidens' cry for their lost purity produces in Teiresias an aversion to the flesh and the desire to transcend it. While Dante swooned at the realization that earthly passion could engender such boredom in eternity, Teiresias, a more cerebral figure, turned to contemplating the two ways of Augustine and the Buddha, West and East; from his contemplation arises the complicated geography of Part V.

Part IV ("Death by Water") bridges the two ways and their attempted resolution in Part V ("What the Thunder Said"). Part IV originally contained eighty-two lines describing a shipwreck off the New England coast. Pound excised the entire section, leaving intact the remaining ten lines—the *epitaphion* of Phlebas the Phoenician, known today as "Death by Water," the shortest and least discussed part of the poem. It is virtually impossible to read these ten verses without recalling two similar deaths: Palinurus and Misenus in the *Aeneid*.

When Palinurus fell into the sea, carrying the tiller with him, his folly occasioned a brief homily from Aeneas: " 'o nimium caelo et pelago confise sereno,/nudus in ignota, Palinure, iacebis harena' " [" 'For counting/over much on a calm world, Palinurus, / You must lie naked on some unknown shore,' " tr. Fitzgerald] (V, 870–71). "Death by Water" ends on a similarly didactic note: "O you who turn the wheel and look to windward,/Consider Phlebas, who was once handsome and tall as you" (lines 320–21).

A Christian writer often feels the need to reply to his pagan sources. Dante replied to the vague eschatology of *Aeneid* VI with an underworld that tempered scholasticism with fancy; Milton answered the nihilism of the *Lament for Bion* with *Lycidas*. Eliot is replying to the epic convention of the burial of a comrade. The drowned Misenus will experience no rebirth, and the murdered Palinurus will be held by the waves and tossed by the wind (VI, 362). They will give their names to promontories, and their immortality, such as it is, will be the knowledge that Punta di Miseno and Punta di Palinuro bear their names. Eliot is offering an alternative to death by water in ancient epic; water can destroy, but it can also revivify. Phlebas, like Misenus and Palinurus, dies, but he was only the pseudo-Tarot counterpart of Teiresias. In "Death by Water," Eliot kills off Phlebas, almost in the fashion of melodrama, and produces in his place a new Teiresias whose Tarot veneer has been peeled away.

Now the full implications of Madame Sosostris' warning, "Fear death by water," can be seen. The "famous clairvoyante," a wastelander herself, would issue such an admonition, for she regarded death by water, or death by any means, as the ultimate reality, the total cessation of life. Teiresias, who has come to the crossroads of belief where not only two forms of time (horizontal and vertical, man's and God's) intersect but two traditions as well (West and East), knows that death by water is merely death to the world.

Teiresias is now ready to confront a higher power, just as Aeneas was prepared to meet his father in Elysium by his journey of purgation through Hades. "What the Thunder Said" is to *The Waste Land* what the hero's meeting with Anchises is to the *Aeneid*: the poetic as well as the historical climax where suffering becomes destiny and the odyssey of an individual becomes the history of a civilization. It is also in the last part of the poem that Teiresias triumphs over space, a victory he shares with Aeneas. At the close of *Aeneid* VI, the hero has been transported from Hades near Cumae to the Elysian Fields which the Romans identified with the Canary Islands or the unexplored Atlantic. The geography of the *descensus* is the geography of the dream, and Teiresias now finds himself in another continent. The geographical transformation occurs in a series of powerful inversions:

> A woman drew her long black hair out tight
> And fiddled whisper music on those strings
> And bats with baby faces in the violet light
> Whistled, and beat their wings
> And crawled *head downward down* a blackened wall

And *upside down* in air were towers
Tolling reminiscent bells, that kept the hours
And voices singing out of empty cisterns and
    exhausted wells.

(lines 378–85, italics mine)

"What the Thunder Said" also fulfils one of the essentials of the *descensus*: the displacement of the female (Madame Sosostris who speaks through cards) by the male (Prajapati who speaks through thunder). A similar situation occurred in the *Aeneid* where Anchises took over the prophetic function of the Sibyl and unrolled for his son the pageant of Roman history. Prajapati offers no historical review to Teiresias, but only the tripartite command, "Give, Sympathize, Control." There are, of course, literary alternatives to the waste land: a return to purgatory ("*Poi s' ascose nel foco che gli affina'*), metamorphosis ("*Quando fiam uti chelidon* — O swallow swallow"), or the acceptance of a ruined tradition ("*Le Prince d'Aquitaine à la tour abolie*"). But alternatives, as the verses from Kyd suggest, may be little more than escapism through papyrology.

The ambivalent ending of *The Waste Land* where scraps of Western literature are blessed by the *Upanishads* is highly Vergilian. After his meeting with Anchises, Aeneas and the Sibyl left for the upper world through the gate of ivory from which false dreams come to men. Generations of readers have wondered why Vergil chose this gate and not the gate of true dreams, the gate of horn. Like Portia's gold casket in *The Merchant of Venice*, the gate of ivory is deceptive: Vergil has Aeneas leave through the *porta eburna* to suggest that Roman history as yet has only the semblance of greatness. Only in the underworld where memory and desire, past and future are mingled can the true nature of the Roman Empire be seen.

Vergil's twin gates (*geminae portae*) become Eliot's West and East. Eliot has again answered the Classics, but he does not ascribe truth to the East and illusion to the West; the way up and the way down are the same.

T. S. Eliot and the Carthaginian Peace

Eleanor Cook

The Waste Land requires three maps for its place-names. One is a map of Greater London and the lower Thames, for the poem is a London poem even in its final form. One early plan, as Hugh Kenner has argued, conceived of Part III as a vision of London through various Augustan modes, making of the city almost another character, and suggesting a geographical unity as focal point for the poem. At this stage, says Kenner, "the rest of the poem seems to have been planned around it [Part III], guided by the norms and decorums of an Augustan view of history." Then Eliot wrote Part V, the vision of an urban apocalypse became dominant, and Part III was cut accordingly.

The Waste Land is not only a London poem; it is also a European poem, or more precisely a Mediterranean poem. It was always so through the early drafts, and it became noticeably so when, in Part V, London was listed as the last in a series of five great cities, Jerusalem, Athens, Alexandria, Vienna, London. The poem therefore requires a second map for those place-names that are not from the London area, leaving aside the names of Ganga and the Himavant. If those place-names are plotted on a map, they may be seen to ring the Mediterranean in the following sense. The northerly names are not seen as centers, in the way our twentieth-century eyes see them. Rather, they balance Carthage and Mylae to the south, and Jerusalem

---

From *ELH* 46, no. 2 (Summer 1979). © 1979 by The Johns Hopkins University Press.

and Smyrna (now Izmir) to the east. This map coincides roughly with the Roman Empire at its most expansive, and therefore also coincides roughly with the theater of war during World War I. The center of this second map is Rome.

This leaves us with the names of Ganga and the Himavant. The map that is useful here is a very simple and a very symmetrical one: it is Dante's map of the inhabited world. The exact center of this world is Jerusalem. Ninety degrees to the east is the eastern limit, the mouths of the Ganges, which is also the eastern limit of *The Waste Land*. Ninety degrees to the west is the western limit, Gibraltar or the western end of the Mediterranean, which is also the western limit of *The Waste Land*. Precisely halfway between Gibraltar and Jerusalem is Rome. We have thus three maps, one of a city, one of an empire, one of a world. They are not set side by side; that is, we do not make orderly progression from one map to the next in the poem. Rather, it is as if they were layered, and we read meaning from one map into another. Urban vision, imperial vision, world vision: each illuminates the other.

The English Augustans, Mr. Kenner observes, saw encouraging parallels between their London and Rome at the time of Augustus. Eliot's early plan for *The Waste Land*, mentioned above, was to develop satiric parallels between modern London and Augustan London. Mr. Kenner argues persuasively that Eliot "may well have had in mind at one time a kind of modern *Aeneid*, the hero crossing seas to pursue his destiny, detained by one woman and prophesied to by another, and encountering visions of the past and the future, all culminated in a city both founded and yet to be founded, unreal and oppressively real, the Rome through whose past Dryden saw London's future." London was to be "the original Fisher King as well as the original Waste Land, resembling Augustine's Carthage as Dryden's London had resembled Ovid's Rome." With the final revisions, however, the center of the poem became "the urban apocalypse, the great City dissolved into a desert . . ."

But I wonder whether the preeminent pattern for London from first to last was not Rome. Of course, in one sense all the cities in the final version of *The Waste Land* are the same: they are Cities of Destruction. But the poem nonetheless focuses on one particular city, London. Similarly, I think that the poem focuses on one prototype for London, and that the prototype is Rome, the center of the second map, and the center of the western half of the third map. Among these three maps, studies of *The Waste Land* have tended to concentrate on the first and the third, Eliot's urban vision and his world vision. But London in 1922 was still the center of an empire. What I want to concentrate on here is Eliot's vision of imperial apocalypse in *The Waste Land*, working from the hypothesis that a vision of Rome and the Roman Empire lies behind Eliot's vision of London and the British Empire.

Rome could provide a pattern for London in *The Waste Land* for good reason. The most obvious is that Rome was once both a great city and the capital of a great empire. In this, she is no different from those other great cities in Part V that were also capitals of great though very different empires: "Jerusalem, Athens, Alexandria, / Vienna, London." This list is worth examining. Eliot preserves the chronological order of the flourishing of each empire. He lists three ancient empires in one line, two modern ones in the following line. The large gap between the three ancient and two modern empires is dominated by Rome, who—and here she differs from the other cities—held sway over all three old empires. The name of Vienna, capital of the Austro-Hungarian Empire, suggests a line of succession, for the Austro-Hungarian Empire saw itself as heir to the Holy Roman Empire, which in turn saw itself as heir to the Roman Empire. Eliot was explicit about part of this line of succession in 1951:

> For Virgil's conscious mind, it [destiny] means the *imperium romanum*. . . . I think that he had few illusions and that he saw clearly both sides of every question—the case for the loser as well as the case for the winner. . . . And do you really think that Virgil was mistaken? You must remember that the Roman Empire was transformed into the Holy Roman Empire. What Virgil proposed to his contemporaries was the highest ideal even for an unholy Roman Empire, for any merely temporal empire. We are all, so far as we inherit the civilization of Europe, still citizens of the Roman Empire. . . . It remains an ideal, but one which Virgil passed on to Christianity to develop and to cherish.

This is the older Eliot speaking. The younger Eliot was quite detached about Christianity, but Eliot always saw himself as heir to the riches of classical civilization, and especially Roman civilization. "Tradition and the Individual Talent" appeared in 1919, and in 1923 Eliot wrote in the *Criterion*: "If everything derived from Rome were withdrawn—everything we have from Norman-French society, from the Church, from Humanism, from every channel direct and indirect, what would be left? A few Teutonic roots and husks. England is a 'Latin' country . . . " (*Criterion*, 2 [October 1923]).

"For at least seven years, it would seem," writes Kenner, "an urban apocalypse had haunted Eliot's imagination." To an imagination thus haunted, and brooding from 1919 onward over material for what was to be *The Waste Land*, it might very well have appeared that the inheritance of Rome was disintegrating. "I am all for empires," wrote Eliot in January of 1924, "especially the Austro-Hungarian Empire." But the Austro-Hungarian Empire had just been broken up by the Treaty of Versailles in 1919. And Christianity, considered simply as a force in history in the way Henry Adams saw it, might also be disintegrating. "The struggle of 'liberal' against 'orthodox' faith is out of date," Eliot wrote as early as 1916. "The present conflict is far more momentous than that." The ghost of Rome prevails in *The Waste Land* because Rome evolved from the greatest of Western empires into a Christian one; because the various European empires that followed Rome, all the way down to the British Empire, retained something of this inheritance, including the association of church and state (at least, officially); and because Eliot at the time of *The Waste Land* sees the possibility that this inheritance and this association will come to an end in the disintegration of church and state and civilization as we know them. "Eliot . . . once said to me," [Stephen] Spender recalls, "that *The Waste Land* could not have been written at any moment except when it was written—a remark which, while biographically true in regard to his own life, is also true of the poem's time in European history after World War I. The sense that Western civilization was in a state which was the realization of historic doom lasted from 1920 to 1926."

The decline of Western civilization and the parallel between Roman and modern civilization: this suggests Spengler. We tend to associate *The Waste Land* with Spengler, in general because of this sense of the decline of civilization, and in particular because Spengler's seasonal cycle so neatly fits Eliot's allusions to English literature in Parts I to IV of the poem. But Eliot's view of history in *The Waste Land* seems to me less Spengler's than that of Henry Adams, though Stuart Hughes reminds us in his *Oswald Spengler* that the Adams brothers were precursors of Spengler. (Eliot's own dismissal of Spengler is brisk: "These are only a few of the questions suggested by

Mr Perry's work; which compels more attention, I think, than the work of such abstract philosophers of history as Otto [*sic*] Spengler.") In *The Education of Henry Adams*, Adams argues that Christianity is the last great force that the West has known, but that its strength is coming to an end. The twentieth century will see a major shift in civilization, like the last major shift, which began at about the time of Augustine. For Spengler, the modern cycle begins in 900 A.D., Augustine is not a pivotal figure as he is for Adams, and Christianity is not the latest force the West has known. Our age, according to Spengler, parallels that of the shift from Greek to Roman dominance in the Mediterranean, and we are at the beginning of another "Roman" age. "*Rome*, with its rigorous realism—uninspired, barbaric, disciplined, practical, Protestant, *Prussian*—will always give us, working as we must by analogies, the key to understanding our own future." Adams makes no such forecasts, being altogether more tentative, at least in *The Education*. But within what Eliot called the "sceptical patrician," there lay a strong sense of apocalypse. Augustine's *Confessions* do not lie behind *The Education of Henry Adams* for nothing. In 1919, Eliot wrote a review of *The Education of Henry Adams* in which he makes no mention of Adam's view of history. But then, he makes no mention of the Maryland spring, which finds a place in *Gerontion*. (Odd that Eliot says, "there is nothing to indicate that Adams's senses either flowered or fruited," while his subconscious tucked away that sensual, flowering Maryland spring for poetic use.) Nor does he mention Adams's image of the Hudson and the Susquehanna, perhaps the Potomac, and the Seine rising to drown the gods of Walhalla, nor the argument that the *Götterdämmerung* was understood better in New York or in Paris than in Bayreuth. Yet in *The Waste Land* Wagner's Rhine-daughters from the *Götterdämmerung* are given equivalents in the Thames, and it may be that Adams suggested to Eliot the usefulness of the *Götterdämmerung* in a poem about the end of things and about (in part) the life of a river. For Adams, the beginning of the end of the Roman Empire was the beginning of the age we know, and the coming change will not be the end of things, and thus not a true apocalypse. But his imagery and his sense of cataclysm are such that they would have fed an imagination already haunted by the theme of apocalypse.

So would Conrad, and so possibly would Henry James, two writers whom Eliot read and admired. Conrad, of course; enters into *The Waste Land*. Neither James in *The Golden Bowl* nor Conrad in

Heart of Darkness looks ahead like Adams to a change in civilization such as the world has not seen in some fifteen centuries. But both books present a dark and troubled vision of empire, and both make use of a parallel between Rome and London. Here are the opening sentences of *The Golden Bowl*:

> The Prince had always liked his London, when it had come to him; he was one of the Modern Romans who find by the Thames a more convincing image of the truth of the ancient state than any they have left by the Tiber. Brought up on the legend of the City to which the world paid tribute, he recognised in the present London much more than in contemporary Rome the real dimensions of such a case. If it was a question of an *Imperium*, he said to himself, and if one wished, as a Roman, to recover a little the sense of that, the place to do so was on London Bridge.

Parallels between Rome and London were common enough at the turn of the century, but only rarely did they serve to set a question-mark against the enterprise of empire itself, its uses as well as its abuses, its civilization as well as its corruption. Both *The Golden Bowl* and *Heart of Darkness* do this, though Conrad's reaction to the kind of power that underlies the rhetoric of empire is beyond even James's darkness: it is horror. Conrad offers us an ancient Roman view of Londinium at the beginning of *Heart of Darkness*, and a parallel between contemporary London and ancient Rome is implicit. His red-sailed barges in the Thames are also from the beginning of *Heart of Darkness*, and they are already present in the early drafts of Part III of *The Waste Land*.

Something of the force of Conrad's great dark vision of empire on Eliot's imagination in 1919 may be seen in a review of Kipling that Eliot published two weeks before his review of *The Education of Henry Adams*. In 1941, when Eliot wrote an introduction to his selection of Kipling's poems, he outlined sympathetically Kipling's idea of empire. It was for Kipling "not merely an idea . . . it was something the reality of which he felt." And Eliot went on to analyze Kipling's sense of the Empire as an awareness of responsibility. But not in 1919. Then, his reaction to Kipling's imperialism was con-temptuous, and his sympathies clearly lay with Conrad, who pro-vides the contrast to Kipling in the 1919 review.

Both of the poets [Kipling and Swinburne] have a few simple ideas. If we deprecate any philosophical complications, we may be allowed to call Swinburne's Liberty and Mr. Kipling's Empire "ideas." They are at least abstract, and not material which emotion can feed long upon. And they are not (in passing) very dissimilar. Swinburne had the Risorgimento, and Garibaldi, and Mazzini, and the model of Shelley, and the recoil from Tennyson, and he produced Liberty. Mr. Kipling, the Anglo-Indian, had frontier welfare, and rebellions, and Khartoum, and he produced the Empire. And we remember Swinburne's sentiments toward the Boers: he wished to intern them all. Swinburne and Mr. Kipling have these and such concepts; some poets, like Shakespeare or Dante or Villon, and some novelists, like Mr. Conrad, have, in contrast to ideas or concepts, points of view, or "worlds"—what are incorrectly called "philosophies." Mr. Conrad is very germane to the question, because he is in many ways the antithesis of Mr. Kipling. He is, for one thing, the antithesis of Empire (as well as of democracy); his characters are the denial of Empire, of Nation, of Race almost, they are fearfully alone with the Wilderness. Mr. Conrad has no ideas, but he has a point of view, a "world"; it can hardly be defined, but it pervades his work and is unmistakable. It could not be otherwise. Swinburne's and Mr. Kipling's ideas could be otherwise. Had Mr. Kipling taken Liberty and Swinburne the Empire, the alteration would be unimportant.

And that is why both Swinburne's and Mr. Kipling's verse in spite of the positive manner which each presses to his service, appear to lack cohesion—to be, frankly, immature. There is no point of view to hold them together.

Eliot is here working out the function of ideas as against the function of a point of view. (The distinction had appeared already in 1918 in his analysis of Henry James, the analysis that includes the well-known sentence: "He had a mind so fine that no idea could violate it.") But there is no doubt about Eliot's opinion of Kipling's idea as idea. In the later essay, it is Eliot's reaction to that idea that has changed.

This time, he compares Kipling not with Swinburne, but with Dryden, "one other great English writer who put politics into verse."

There is another work that I think entered into the making of *The Waste Land*. It is a book contemporary with the poem; it sheds light on some of the allusions in *The Waste Land*, ties the poem to post–World War I history, and incidentally relates Eliot's work at Lloyd's Bank to his poetry. It treats the theme of imperial collapse, and it uses Rome as an implicit example. It is John Maynard Keynes's *The Economic Consequences of the Peace*.

Eliot in 1951 observed that Virgil knew the case for the loser as well as the case for the winner. When he cut and revised the drafts of *The Waste Land*, he deleted several references to Virgil. The one specific reference he chose to retain is an allusion to Dido, a reference that stresses the price rather than the glory of empire. Virgil's Sibyl of Cumae knew the price of empire, too. (Mr. Kenner notes that we are meant to recall Virgil's Sibyl, if we have any sibylline knowledge at all, when we see the ruined Sibyl of Cumae in the poem's epigraph.) In Book VI of the *Aeneid*, the Sibyl of Cumae warns Aeneas of the realities on which empires are founded: *bella, horrida bella et Thybrim multo spumentem sanguine cerno*. And the Tiber, running with blood, takes its place behind the great rivers of the poem, Cleopatra's Nile, the Rhine so recently also running with blood, the Thames. Beyond that, it merges into the larger bodies of water that provided routes for the great maritime empires. All the cities of Part V are associated with famous waters. And the great maritime empire of 1922, on which the sun never set, has behind her the great maritime empire of Rome, and behind that the greatest (we are told) maritime empire of them all, Phoenicia's, whose sailors and ships were a source of power for centuries, and a byword for good seamanship. (One of her sailors appears in Part I and Part IV of *The Waste Land*.) At the naval battle of Mylae in the First Punic War, her erstwhile colony Carthage was defeated by Rome. In the Second and Third Punic Wars, she was again defeated; in the Third War, Carthage was besieged, and when the city had been taken, her citizens were slaughtered, the city levelled and sown with salt in order to make the soil sterile, and the site dedicated to the infernal gods. The Carthage to which Augustine came was a rebuilt Carthage.

The phrase "a Carthaginian Peace" would therefore mean a peace settlement so punitive as to destroy the enemy entirely and even to make sterile the land on which he lives. What it does to the victor is another question. In December 1919, John Maynard Keynes published his book *The Economic Consequences of the Peace*, in which he passionately denounced the Treaty of Versailles as a "Carthaginian Peace." (He had resigned as representative of the British Treasury at the Peace Conference.) The book was widely read (according to Etienne Mantoux's *The Carthaginian Peace*, it had been translated into eleven languages and sold some 140,000 copies by 1924), and whether or how far the peace treaties were a Carthaginian Peace was widely disputed. Eliot, as the Lloyd's representative "in charge of settling all the pre-War Debts between the Bank and the Germans, 'an important appointment, full of interesting legal questions', . . . was kept busy 'trying to elucidate knotty points in that appalling document the Peace Treaty.' " It is unlikely he would not have read Keynes; he would certainly have known the argument of the book. (In a "London Letter" in the *Dial* for March 1921, Eliot referred to the "respect . . . with which Clemenceau and Lloyd George bonified President Wilson." The view of the respect and bonifying among the three men is Keynes's view, though the remark hardly proves Eliot had read Keynes's book. Nor does Eliot's later remark, cited above, "I am all for empires, especially the Austro-Hungarian Empire," though the view of the Austro-Hungarian Empire is also Keynes's.) [Author's Note: Evidence that Eliot read *The Economic Consequences of the Peace* may be found in the *New English Weekly* 29, no. 5 (May 16, 1946), pp. 47–48. I am grateful to Christopher Ricks for drawing this to my attention.]

The phrasing in *The Economic Consequences of the Peace* evokes an apocalyptic foreboding and sense of nightmare very like that in *The Waste Land*. Keynes wrote that he himself came to be "haunted by other and more dreadful specters. Paris was a nightmare, and everyone there was morbid. A sense of impending catastrophe overhung the frivolous scene . . . the mingled significance and unreality of decisions. . . . The proceedings of Paris all had this air of extraordinary importance and unimportance at the same time. The decisions seemed charged with consequences to the future of human society; yet the air whispered that the word was not flesh, that it was futile, insignificant, of no effect, dissociated from events." In the "hot, dry room in the President's house . . . the Four fulfilled their destinies in empty and arid intrigue." Clemenceau, "dry in soul and empty of hope, very old and tired," schemed on behalf of the "policy of an old man, whose most vivid impressions and most lively imagination are of the past and not of the future." Paris was a "morass," its atmosphere "hot and poisoned," its halls "treacherous." "Then began the weaving of that web of sophistry and Jesuitical exegesis. . . ." "In this autumn of 1919, in which I write, we are at the dead season of our fortunes. . . . Our power of feeling or caring beyond the immediate questions of our own material well-being is temporarily eclipsed." This is not Pound speaking, or Hesse: it is Keynes, who supports his plea with pages of detailed economic argument that would have interested Eliot professionally. ("I want to find out something about the science of money while I am at it: it is an extraordinarily interesting subject," Eliot wrote to his mother on April 11, 1917, just after joining Lloyd's. And to Lytton Strachey on June 1, 1919: "You are very—ingenuous—if you can conceive me conversing with rural deans in the cathedral close. I do not go to cathedral towns but to centres of industry. My thoughts are absorbed in questions more important than ever enters the heads of deans—as *why* it is cheaper to buy steel bars from America than from Middlesbrough, and the probable effect—the exchange difficulties with Poland—and the appreciation of the rupee.")

Ezra Pound saw London as another Carthage: "London has just escaped from the First World War, but it is certain to be destroyed by the next one, because it is in the hands of the international financiers. The very place of it will be sown with salt, as Carthage was, and forgotten by men; or it will be sunk under water." But in 1922, I think Eliot saw London as primarily another Rome, who had brought a famous trading enemy to her knees. Cleanth Brooks, commenting on the use of Mylae in *The Waste Land*, notes that the "Punic War was a trade war—might be considered a rather close parallel to our late war." And Keynes quotes Clemenceau's view that England in the First World War, as in each preceding century, had destroyed a trade rival. The poem's one-eyed merchant and Mr. Eugenides from Smyrna with his shorthand trading terms are figures of importance in an empire. "Money is, after all, life blood," Spender reminds us. The sense of doom in the twenties "emanated from the revolutionary explosions and still more from the monetary collapse of central Europe." Carthage is in *The Waste Land* not only because of its connections with Dido and Aeneas, *The Tempest*, and St. Augustine; not only as a colony of Phoenicia, Phoenicia who had given the Greeks most of their alphabet, which in turn was given to the Romans (by Greeks at Cumae, say Crosby and Schaffer); not only as part of a great maritime empire. It is in the poem also because Carthage is for Rome the great rival, as she is at the beginning of the *Aeneid*, and the relations between the two a pattern for enmity so established that Keynes could use the phrase "a Carthaginian Peace" without further explanation. The argument for declaring the third war against Carthage (repeated again and again by Cato the Censor, with his famous refrain *Carthago delenda est*) was the argument at the center of the controversy over the peace treaties: whether the reviving prosperity of a defeated trade rival could become a danger to the victor. In a poem of 1922, to introduce the battle of Mylae where the reader expects a reference to a World War I battle is to raise chilling questions. The line out of Baudelaire's Paris, which follows the spectral Mylae speech and ends Part I, does not help either, for those who had read Keynes: "You! hypocrite lecteur!—mon semblable,—mon frère!"

For a Carthaginian peace is one that slowly but surely deflects back upon the victor. It is a common argument that Roman life began to decline after the Punic wars. As long as Rome was in a state of war, Augustine writes near the beginning of *The City of God*, she could maintain concord and high standards of civic life. "But after the destruction of Carthage," he continues, quoting Sallust, "there came the highest pitch of discord, greed, ambition, and all the evils which generally spring up in times of prosperity" (II.18). The argument was repeated by Lecky in 1877: "complete dissolution of Roman morals began shortly after the Punic wars" (*OED*, "Punic," A.1). Keynes similarly argues his case as much on behalf of the victors as the vanquished: "they [France and Italy] invite their own destruction also, being so deeply and inextricably intertwined with their victims by hidden psychic and economic bonds." "If we aim deliberately at the impoverishment of Central Europe, . . . nothing can then delay for very long that final civil war . . . which will destroy, whoever is victor, the civilization and progress of our generation." For Rome the victor, and so long the victor that she must have seemed invincible, the eventual turn of time brings Alaric and Attila. Rome itself experiences destruction. St. Augustine, who telescopes history much as Eliot does, argues that the destruction of Rome is only fitting, for the outward devastation only matches the collapse of the inner fabric of society. "For in the ruin of our city it was stone and timber which fell to the ground; but in the lives of those Romans we saw the collapse not of material but of moral defences, not of material but of spiritual grandeur. The lust that burned in their hearts was more deadly than the flame which consumed their dwellings" (II.1). This is true not only of public life, but also of private. "Now a man's house ought to be the beginning, or rather a small component part of the city, and every beginning is directed to some end of its own kind. . . . domestic peace contributes to the peace of the city" (XIX.16).

No argument that Rome provides the preeminent pattern for London in *The Waste Land* can ignore the classic exposition of the *civitas Romae* and the *civitas Dei*, Augustine's *City of God*. Spender speaks of the implicit contrast in *The Waste Land* of the two cities, and he is surely right about this. The original drafts twice included references to an ideal city, though in the end Eliot omitted any explicit reminder of a *civitas Dei*. One reference was in Part III, and read as follows: "Not here, O Glaucon [originally Ademantus], but in another world" (l. 120), which is annotated in Valerie Eliot's edition of the drafts of the poem: "Adeimantus and Glaucon, brothers of Plato, were two of the interlocutors in *The Republic*. Appalled by his vision of the "Unreal City," Eliot may be alluding to the passage (Book IX, 592 A-B) which inspired the idea of the City of God among Stoics and Christians, and found its finest exponent in St. Augustine." As the poem's shape changed, the ideal city shifted. In a draft of the speech of Madame Sosostris in Part I, the following line is inserted in a bracket after the present line 56: "I John saw these things, and heard them"; the quotation, from near the end of Revelation, refers not only to John's vision of judgment, but more particularly to his vision of the New Jerusalem, which immediately precedes it. Eliot finally cut all references to an ideal city, because, I think, the developing theme of urban and imperial apocalypse refused to accommodate so firm a hope as that in *The Republic* or Revelation. What Eliot kept from the Johannine vision was the dark view of the earthly city or Babylon. The sense of an impending *dies irae* hangs over most of his poem.

Augustine's earthly city is of course Babylon also, together with Babylon's daughter, Rome (*Babylonia, quasi prima Roma . . . ipsa Roma quasi secunda Babylonia* [XVIII.2]). And over Augustine's earthly city, the *civitas Romae*, there also hangs a sense of doom in *The City of God*. Rome had been forewarned of her destruction, writes Augustine, by Sibylline prophecy, and the same prophecies warn her of the final apocalypse. Augustine is one of the Church fathers responsible for the conversion of Virgil's Sibyl into Christian prophetess, and, if Virgil's Sibyl of Cumae lives behind the Sibyl of Cumae in *The Waste Land*, so also, I think, may the later Christian Sibyl. "The Sibyl of Erythrae or, as some are inclined to believe, of Cumae . . . is evidently to be counted among those who belong to the City of God," writes Augustine (XVIII.24). And he goes on to quote in full the Sibylline oracle which prophesies a day of judgment, using sources from both the Old and New Testaments, the oracle especially famed because its initial letters form an acrostic in Greek that spells "fish," one of the common symbols for Christ in the early Church. There are other fates for the Sibyl than the fate Petronius portrayed and Eliot quoted, though they offer no comfort to the inhabitant or the reader of *The Waste Land*. The Sibyl may find her way into the words of the *dies irae* (*teste David cum Sibylla*), and her verses may be called the fifteen signs of the judgment and sung in some places as late as 1549. Whatever evidence is chosen, this Sibyl is associated with the collapse of Rome and also with the final apocalypse and the day of judgment. In 1921, Eliot was considering poetic treatments of the day of judgment at least enough to make clear how not to treat it: some poets, he wrote in the Spring issue of *Tyro*, "could imagine the Last Judgment only as a lavish display of Bengal lights, Roman candles, catherine wheels, and inflammable fire-balloons. *Vous, hypocrite lecteur. . . .*"

Eliot's dark vision of the earthly city may be close to Augustine's dark vision of the *civitas Romae*, but it goes without saying that for Augustine the activities associated with any Fisher King, like those in *The Waste Land*, would be evidence only of superstition. *The City of God* includes references to such activities only to attack them. The belief, for example, that the Delphic Apollo might have inflicted sterility upon the land is mere superstition (XVIII.12); so are fears of an evil spell cast upon the land that motivate the fertility rites (VII.24). It is likewise superstition that inspires the familiar proverb, *Pluuia defit, causa Christiani sunt* ("No rain! It's all the fault of the Christians" [II.3]). Welldon's edition of *The City of God* notes that Augustine makes use of this proverb frequently, and it is a proverb that, read with varying degrees of irony, may be applied very handily to *The Waste Land*.

In an apocalyptic mode, the world may seem split into the sweetness of a visionary, ideal and virtually unattainable world, and the sordidness of an actual, present, and virtually inescapable world.

There is no middle ground, and practical, temporal concerns and governance are left to others. This kind of painful contrast is what gives *The Waste Land* its poignancy. It is the viewpoint of someone not at home in the world, a peregrine, like Augustine. Augustine was an outsider in more than one sense: not only was his overwhelming allegiance given to another world, but he was a provincial in the Roman Empire, one of the *peregrini* or resident aliens during his stay in Milan. In *The Waste Land*, he takes his place among those other great exiles or provincials who perhaps understood their city and their empire all the better for having been exiles or provincials: Ezekiel, Ovid, Dante. And Eliot? One of Eliot's quotations is from the psalm of exile, with its passionate love of Jerusalem, and its cry, "How shall we sing the Lord's song in a strange land?" The cry echoes behind the homeless voices of *The Waste Land*.

But the Jewish voices were able to utter this psalm or to include an Ezekiel. In the twentieth century, there remain only fragmented voices, a desiccated Sibyl. The apocalyptic mode in *The Waste Land* moves toward its own destruction in the disintegration of the uses of language. Augustine, whose etymology is highly idiosyncratic, thought that the name Babylon was connected with the name Babel. Babylon may thus also be called "confusion," and "punishment in the form of a change of language" is the fate of a Babel or of any Babylon or of any Rome—a punishment which some readers may feel Eliot demonstrates with peculiar force. (Another twentieth-century example of this punishment had been seen at the Peace Conference, where the difficulties of negotiating had been compounded by the fact that only Clemenceau, among the Four, spoke both French and English.)

The dangers of abandoning the middle ground of practical, temporal affairs are all too apparent. At the end of *The Waste Land*, there is a turning, or rather a returning, toward this middle earth, and away from exile or private grief. The apocalyptic mode is useful but not for long. It provides an ideal but no working pattern for living in this world. A working pattern without an ideal may very well collapse sooner or later, but an ideal with no working pattern can find terrible ways to translate itself into action, or can find itself readily outmanoeuvred and paralysed. Augustine does not ignore the question of how to live in the earthly city. And Keynes, at the end of *The Economic Consequences of the Peace*, tempers his own dark vision with practical suggestions for relieving the nightmare.

The Waste Land, in the end, retains its geographical unity, but the unity becomes far more complex. London as a city forms one focal point. The maps shift, as we muse on the poem, and London becomes a center of empire, another Rome. Do they ever shift again, so that London and Rome become Jerusalem, the center of Dante's world? Never, in the old sense, and not until *Little Gidding* in a mystical sense, and by this time the center may be anywhere, "England and nowhere. Never and always."

The Structure and Mythical Method of *The Waste Land*

Grover Smith

Eliot, devouring his experience of the current cultural season, proved his point about poetry—that anything whatever might find a place in it (*Selected Essays*). His "long" poem at all stages was made of a great variety of moments of thought and feeling. The poem shown to Pound and preserved in the *Facsimile* included subordinate poems, afterwards removed, the material having occurred in various forms and at different times. Some commentators therefore deny the integrity of the work which they choose to consider a mere assemblage. They assume that *The Waste Land* fails to combine its parts, and they criticise it on the superficial principle that a poem consisting only of scenes or vignettes or flashes of imagery has no unified structure. Yet *The Waste Land* in its structure achieves two kinds of unity, the one psychological, the other cultural or "mythic." Nor was it made of random materials. On the one hand its details focus intensities for a single point of view, and on the other they were filtered and transformed. They passed through a mind, they expressed thereby a "personal world" of outward form. Critics who doubt the unity of the poem but who acknowledge it as poetry (for example, Aiken, 1923, and less favourably Kenner, 1959) have produced descriptions of it with more than curiosity value, though impaired by an obstinately false conception of it—one impatient with the poet and his *donnée* as well. The fallacy of the notion that *The Waste Land* should be re-

From *The Waste Land*. © 1983 by Grover Smith. Allen & Unwin, 1983. Originally entitled "*The Waste Land* in the Making."

garded, with various shades of implication, as a set of diversities, is that it sidesteps the evidence. All art is in some measure heterogeneously composed, and certainly it is possible for a work to fall short of unifying itself. But, though the structure of *The Waste Land* presents the difficulty of the unconventional, and is not obvious, it is certainly visible in the poem and is moreover explicit in the *prose* part of the poem, the "Notes."

The chief of the critics to doubt the structural order of *The Waste Land* was Eliot himself; but it is necessary to understand that the Eliot who repudiated it was the Eliot of the 1950s, severing himself from his own past and yet not going so far as to amend the poetic text belonging to the past. Self-criticism which would substitute hindsight for past vision is like historical revisionism. In both cases a new *historian* appears, but the things that happened in the past happened nevertheless. In his *Paris Review* interview (1959) Eliot was asked whether *The Waste Land* was changed in "intellectual structure" by Pound's "excisions," and to this he replied: "No, I think it was just as structureless, only in a more futile way, in the longer version." The answer did not do justice to the question; but it is not the questioner's dissociation of "intellectual" from other structure that proves my point but Eliot's dismissal of all structure even in the original poem, which he had not seen in more than a third of a century and would never see again. Neither "version," that is, had more or less or any kind of structure. His refusal to compare cut discussion off. This may not have happened on purpose, but even so it served as a defence; and Eliot never liked to answer in depth for his poetic intentions. Also the question, as asked, could have involved on the one side, or its answer could have involved on the other, some criticism of Pound's intervention. He would have wished to defend Pound. But it is possible to detect hyperbole in what he said. There certainly had been structure to *The Waste Land*, call it intellectual or not; but Eliot could no longer *feel* the structural idea in satisfactory terms. Once he would have defended in private the structure he had conceived, just as he would have defended his "Notes," which a few years earlier (1956) he derogated in "The Frontiers of Criticism" as "bogus scholarship" (*On Poetry and Poets*). That structure, indeed, he modified insignificantly as he composed, but it endures. To dismiss the structure was, in the interview, to evade it—because an alternative reply might have necessitated justifications of what Eliot had come to think unjustifiable, a structure he could no longer see. My point, finally, is that his answer is evidence, but that its strict inaccuracy makes it evidence for something contrary to what it says. Eliot had concluded that the structure of *The Waste Land* was a failure. Whether he thought it a failure of conception or of execution is not clear and is not crucial.

The nature of the structure was explained in Eliot's "Notes" to *The Waste Land*, in the description of Tiresias:

> Tiresias, although a mere spectator and not indeed a "character," is yet the most important personage in the poem, uniting all the rest. Just as the one-eyed merchant, seller of currants, melts into the Phoenician Sailor, and the latter is not wholly distinct from Ferdinand Prince of Naples, so all the women are one woman, and the two sexes meet in Tiresias. What Tiresias *sees*, in fact, is the substance of the poem.
>
> (Note to line 218)

The structural order envisaged through the spectator—unifier function, far from being vague, has a visible logic, and it is at least as cogent as most innovations of modern art. This order is reinforced somewhat more in cancelled passages than in the shorter version of *The Waste Land*, by an autobiographical parallel; the cancelled epigraph from Conrad's *Heart of Darkness* also hints at this. (See Preface, above.) The spectator function, but not the unifier effect, recalls what years ago I referred to as a Proustian element in *The Waste Land*, meaning the presence of a consciousness engaged in sifting over the past, as in *À la recherche du temps perdu*. In stream-of-consciousness writing, time in one or another way undergoes dislocation. Sometimes different time segments are abruptly brought together, as in Ford Madox Ford's time-shift novels; sometimes they are commingled indiscriminately, as in Molly Bloom's soliloquy in *Ulysses*. When, by some convention of temporal transcendence, the consciousness is made to dislocate or rearrange *historical* events, or especially to blend together scenes or incidents from different ages, it becomes a literary Absolute, a cosmic consciousness. In *The Waste Land* Tiresias is the spectator of his private past and also of the universal past. The poem depicts a palimpsest or layered mixture of historical times. It does this partly by means of literary juxtapositions and sometimes by tricking out the present in a literary style imitated from the past. The time mixture fits neatly with the unifier function of Tiresias; for as he contemplates (and, being the poet, stylistically renders) various times he enters into the personages who populate them. Though a point of resemblance between the Phoenician Sailor and Ferdinand Prince of Naples is not immediately apparent (they both sail on ships?), one may accept such mergers of identity on the principle that in a dreamlike vision people equal to the same people are equal to each other.

Now these several strategies with time, literary style and personalities have precedents in Joyce's *Ulysses*: the first in the parallel with the *Odyssey*, the next in the extravagant recapitulation of style in "Oxen of the Sun," and the last in the confused shape-shiftings of "Circe." Hugh Kenner in his essay "The Urban Apocalypse" has suggested that Eliot, through a succession of references to Virgil's *Aeneid* in the poem, may have thought at some point of creating a modern quest of Aeneas as Joyce had created that of Bloom—Odysseus. The clue to this quest, which can be made to work in reading the poem mythologically, is the descent into hell, as has been demonstrated by Bernard F. Dick in an article entitled *"The Waste Land and the Descensus ad Inferos."* Kenner connects Virgil with *The Waste Land* in a different way. He surmises that after reading Van Doren's *John Dryden*, with its express comparison of the London of the 1660s and 1670s to the Rome of Ovid, Eliot converted the familiar analogy expressed by the term "Augustan" to the service of a thematic and stylistic interplay between modern and Augustan London. For the theme of the city in the original section of his poem, "The Fire Sermon," the obvious epical parallels were those provided by the *Aeneid*, which Dryden translated, the epic that looks to the founding of Rome. Kenner's hypothesis constricts Eliot's project unduly at its inception; Eliot had much more in mind, but he may also have had this. Van Doren would have been tickled to think that his book had affected *The Waste Land*. Whether Dryden's impact was so forcible, the hard evidence does not establish. Nor do the Augustan literary modes predominate in "The Fire Sermon." Eliot drew upon Van Doren's book for some details of the section, these being from Dryden indeed, as I [show elsewhere]; and he may have owed to it traces of "the decorums of urban satire" for which Kenner makes claims in "The Urban Apocalypse." Thus the fifteen-line passage beginning "London, the swarming life you kill and breed," ultimately rejected from the work, could have been suggested in part by the long apostrophe to London in Dryden's "The Medal" (lines 167 ff.), a poem not cited by Van Doren or Kenner. Eliot's passage, however, was written in *terza rima*, and the interim cancellations do not show Eliot going over to Dryden's couplets definitely or anticipating the quatrain form of his own succeeding lines. Nothing in the passage sounds much like either Dryden or Dante. Nor despite Kenner, do the quatrains recall Dryden.

The time mixture of the original "Fire Sermon," like that of the poem long familiar, presents dissolving views of a city that is basically modern London but melts into its past layers indiscriminately. As a counterpart of Tiresias' consciousness, this has one structural value; as a treatment of historical time, another. The time mixture however makes no sharp distinction in this respect. It and Tiresias himself are interdependent; they combine in expressing the moral "myth"—that new and surprising distillation towards which the poem aspires as presaged by Eliot's critical hints of 1921. This myth, to objectify its point of view as a vision of good and evil, employs the container as well as the contents, the former a structured identity to compensate for the looseness and variety of the latter. In a solipsistic universe the mind and the external panorama would reduce to a single reality; in a Bradleyan context they could be described as *experience experiencing*. But Eliot's poem, like Proust's vast novel, keeps the two at the arm's length of contemplation. Yet in theory, like facing mirrors magically filled with shadows, their private and social realities reflect each other. Each is the other's self-transformation, each the other's self-judgement.

So conceived in the planning of the "long poem" that began with "The Fire Sermon," Eliot's myth did not depend upon traditional mythology. The difference between making myth and using it is essential to the understanding of *The Waste Land* as a work of art. The two concepts really involve different senses of the term "myth," which in neither sense unfortunately, whether in Eliot's vocabulary or in common usage, has a synonym. The traditional sense carries implications of the primitive, the prelogical, the spellbound and superstitious, interesting to the folklorist and anthropologist. The new sense implies a deliberate effort to reawaken the unconscious and intuitive powers of the primitive myth-maker in the service of poetic feeling; and to create such poetic images of human behaviour as to suggest for the quotidian rituals of modern life a meaning like that provided for less self-conscious society by magic and myth. If in effect the new myth-maker calls upon the same resources of the mind as the primitive one, then in the same sense the structure he presents will mirror the workings of the mind, its psychology. It will, however, conform to an up-to-date psychological model. In *The Waste Land* the psyche is modern, the content miscellaneous, and the controlling mind transformational; all are necessary. The substance of the poem forms a myth, something wholly new, generated by that mind in the semblance of a timeless point of view or continuum, filled with images and echoes and diverse voices. The presence of traditional mythic personages in the formal scheme is not the mythic principle but only an aspect of it.

Such is not what critics have generally understood by the myth in *The Waste Land*. Rather there has been a great to-do about traditional mythic images as formal and moral devices—Tiresias and the Grail figures and the characters in epics, notably those of Virgil and Dante. This emphasis is natural and inevitable, and it will not be neglected in the present account. For, along with modern literature, traditional myths supplied Eliot with the time dimension for his mythic pattern. It is impossible to look at it without looking at them, except at the cost of incomprehension. The received myths of thwarted questing and fruitless psychological initiation (to cite one type of modern reduction applied to them), with their social and religious perspectives, fit indispensably into the spiritual or rather the moral vision of the poem, this also being formulated in traditional images. Thus what Eliot called, in his notes to lines 308–9, the "collocation" of the Buddha and Saint Augustine gives to the title of Part III, "The Fire Sermon," its meaning of hell exposed in the desires of the flesh. Thus too the "burning" metaphor applied by Augustine to sinful Carthage in his *Confessions* (III,1) reinforces the contrasting implication of Eliot's line borrowed, in the original drafts, from the reference to the virtuous city in Plato's *Republic* (XI, 592): "Not here, O Glaucon, but in another world." Through Augustine, as Valerie Eliot comments in the *Facsimile*, Platonic conceptions of the virtuous city were expressed as the City of God. In "The Fire Sermon" as first written, the sinful or "burning" city, Plato's city of the tyrannical, has a visionary complement in the ideal city of the just. These paradigms of the actual and the transcendent afford, then, a moral framework; and the traditional material, mythic and otherwise, reinforces this with its anthropological glosses of fertility and drought. All the while, the framework or matrix is identified with the vision of Tiresias. It is Tiresias who gazes with Augustine upon the city of tyrant *demos*, the populace hungering for sense-gratification and power; who entertains with Plato a dream of wisdom; who, involved in illusion, fails at Buddhist Enlightenment. These experiences are not depicted but synthesised as the old strands are woven into a modern psyche, a myth containing the experiences of a cultural past.

Myth made to the formula of "The Romantic Englishman" can serve to point a moral or construct a morality. But the myths, the traditional legends that adorn the tale or furnish its matter, import uncontrollable significances. To find mythic parallels is to explain nothing; it is to add implications that in their turn beg for explanation. The value of Jessie L. Weston or Sir James Frazer to *The Waste Land* is that each has a coherent system of ritual and myth with which Eliot's may be compared and by which its coherence may be tested. In creating his image of an interior world and projecting it as an outward landscape of events, Eliot made a multiplicity of details into myth different from all other myths. Since it is a point of view it absorbs other points of view into itself—the scholars' coherent interpretations especially, because they are structured as scattered legends are not. This blending process does not imply "taking over" the opinions expressed by scholars of myth; as always when Eliot's poetry borrows, the adoptions form a new equilibrium. So *The Waste Land* is tentative where Weston is doctrinaire, diffuse where Frazer is organised. Even Frazer, Eliot noted in the *Nouvelle Revue française* of 1 November 1923 (vol. 21), tended as his work became more voluminous to avoid more and more explaining his material. This shunning of hypotheses, Eliot commented, was a point of view, a "vision." I do not think this fair to Frazer's scientific commitment, but it can profitably be transferred to *The Waste Land*. In the unpublished paper of 1913 for Royce known as "The Interpretation of Primitive Ritual" (see above), Eliot had criticised the interpretation Frazer offered at the conclusion of *The Dying God* (*The Golden Bough*, vol. 4) of primitive rites of spring. Frazer says that early man conducted spring ceremonies with magical intent and in the belief, mistaken indeed, that by imitating the natural phenomena of fertility he could ensure the annual renewal of those processes upon which his life depended. Looking at the daily course of the sun, the monthly growth and extinction of the moon, the slow seasonal round of the agricultural year, the primitive mind was beset with fears and worries: would the daylight return, would the moon wax again, would the spring blossom once more? "These and a thousand such misgivings," Frazer remarks, "may have thronged the fancy and troubled the peace of the man who first began to reflect on the mysteries of the world he lived in, and to take thought for a more distant future than the morrow" (vol. 4). Primitive man according to Frazer allayed these anxieties by experimenting: magic was one of his experiments in commanding the order of nature, which he conceived as "contagiously" or "sympathetically" bound to respond to his rituals with phenomena resembling their symbolic content. Eliot, fresh from the social psychology of Lucien Lévy-Bruhl, contested Frazer's description. He argued that from Frazer's method of comparing primitive customs it was not possible to arrive at this result; historical and comparative methods could show nothing of the purpose or intention behind a specific ritual. Eliot's point was well taken, and it follows from it that ritual and myth alike, for the same analysis would apply to both, may be products less of primitive logic than of primeval fantasy. Frazer's assumption that the rites of spring arose experimentally from a conception of cause and effect *may* have been correct, but quite as easily the unknown facts may have been otherwise. In reading Eliot's poetry and in particular *The Waste Land*, one should bear in mind that the adoption of certain material from Frazer implies in no way Eliot's outright acceptance of Frazer's interpretations. The anthropological data of *The Golden Bough*, as Eliot regarded that monumental compilation, had perhaps slipped through their interpreter's hands.

Eliot's point of view, never servile to that of others, assimilated that of the literary anthropologists in this respect, that the function they saw in myth helped Eliot express his feelings through myth. They saw that myth, reinforced with ritual, was a way of interpreting experience from another, primitive point of view. He, synthesising his own myth, put in charge of it a consciousness with roots in magic and primitive psychology, but also modern, for it was his own consciousness as a poet. The poet, bringing into play surviving unconscious habits of the mind, reenacts the primitive myth-maker's role. His emotions, out of which he makes art, are the ecstasy and terror which the daylight hours of civilisation relegate to the forgotten darkness. The importance to Eliot of this theme of a symbolic descent into prelogical realms of perception was to be reflected, after he finished the poem and decided to call it *The Waste Land*, in his first choice of an epigraph from Conrad's *Heart of Darkness*. Mr Kurtz in the minds of Conrad's readers remains an explorer of forbidden hells of primitive knowledge. It is to such knowledge that his dying words are directed: "The horror! the horror!" Eliot of course had not read only Frazer and Weston, whose anthropology is comparatively antiseptic. He had read, as [an important article by William Harmon shows], a large assortment of field anthropologists, sociologists and social psychologists; and his interest in their work went back to his days in Royce's seminar. At that early epoch and subsequently, he fastened upon psychology with especial concentration, and above all upon its speculations concerning the primitive stratum of thought. He appealed to this level of himself in turning to myths and mythic invention.

Many critics have seen in Eliot's use of myth what I shall call the "nostalgic" implication. If, so their reasoning runs, primitive life expressed its wholeness, its harmony, in myth and ritual, then Eliot invoked these primitive forms to contrast with them the social sterility of his own time. His longing thus stretched towards a departed age of precivilised cultural vitality, and his dream towards a reawakening of this in religious participation. This implies, evidently, something resembling the primitivism of D. H. Lawrence; but it is untrue to *The Waste Land*, which makes no social presentation compatible with it.

Nostalgia is reserved for the personal domain, for memories of vanished freedom. As *The Waste Land* centres on the sufferings of Eliot in his marriage, on the lost opportunity hinted at in the "Hyacinth garden" passage, it is difficult in the light of the *Facsimile* to recover the attitude of a critical generation which greeted fertility myth and ritual as harbingers of salvation. On the contrary they are to all appearances symbols of lost manhood, for they belong invariably to contexts of frustration. The world of the poem is that of the primal Fall. In his study of the myth of the Fall as it affected nineteenth-century American culture, *The American Adam* (1955), R. W. B. Lewis shows from the literature of the time a persistent concern with the symbolic theme of sin and redemption. The two levels, the personal and the social, interacted variously. But missing from Eliot's postscript to this cultural criticism, visible in the contrary perspectives of Puritan and romantic, is the mechanism of justification. Neither grace nor self-reliance is invoked, only endurance. Some take the closing thrice-repeated "Shantih" as a whisper of hope, but more consistently it may be taken as heavily ironic. If it is hopeful it is the first word of the poem which is. On the artistic level only, the poem works a reverse transformation of Tiresias the blind into Tiresias the all-seeing. For himself he claims nothing but that he has survived.

In order to account for Eliot's adaptations of traditional myth, especially the Grail legend, critics have cited the concluding paragraph of Eliot's review "Ulysses, Order, and Myth" (November 1923), published twenty-one months after the novel appeared. The passage might have been tailored to provoke their observations:

> In using the myth, in manipulating a continuous parallel between contemporaneity and antiquity, Mr. Joyce is pursuing a method which others must pursue after him. They will not be imitators, any more than the scientist who uses the discoveries of an Einstein in pursuing his own, independent, further investigations. It is simply a way of controlling, of ordering, of giving a shape and a significance to the immense panorama of futility and anarchy which is contemporary history. It is a method already adumbrated by Mr Yeats, and of the need for which I believe Mr Yeats to have been the first contemporary to be conscious. It is a method for which the horoscope is auspicious. Psychology (such as it is, and whether our reaction to it be comic or serious), ethnology, and The Golden Bough have concurred to make possible what was impossible even a few years ago. Instead of narrative method, we may now use the mythical method. It is, I seriously believe, a step toward making the modern world possible for art, toward that order and form which Mr Aldington so earnestly desires. And only those who have won their own discipline in secret and without aid, in a world which offers very little assistance to that end, can be of any use in furthering this advance.
>
> (*Dial*, vol. 75)

Richard Aldington, made to kiss the friendly rod in this defence of *Ulysses*, had earlier composed, before the book was published as a whole, an "arranged" critique intended to draw favourable attention to Joyce (*English Review*, vol. 32). But he had blundered by calling Joyce's talent "undisciplined." Eliot, also by "arrangement" rounding upon this imprudent pupil, lectured him on where the discipline lay: in "Mr Joyce's parallel use of the Odyssey." He remarked that this had since been explicated in an article by Valery Larbaud (originally a lecture, published in French in the spring of 1922, and then in English in the *Criterion* of the following October, which also contained *The Waste Land*); and he mentioned Larbaud rather dismissively. Larbaud, primed by Joyce, had talked about Homeric parallels and symbols and had called the *Odyssey* the "key" to *Ulysses*, as accounting for the incidents and characters. More important, and ignored by Eliot, was Larbaud's description of how Joyce focused events through the minds of Bloom and Stephen, so that "the detailed history" of their day, with much else, came over directly instead of being "told . . . in narrative form" (*Criterion*, vol. 1). (This was less than precisely accurate: in *most* of Joyce's chapters stream-of-consciousness effects are accompanied by authorial narration.) Larbaud did not mention myth as such, and did not imply that the parallel to the *Odyssey* replaced narrative or tended in that way. If narrative form was breaking down, this was obviously as a result of Joyce's stylistic distractions and, technically, in his abandonment of it in certain chapters. Eliot, on the other hand, had experienced *Ulysses* as a presage of other inventions, of an upsurge of myth, and he addressed himself to this future in "Ulysses, Order, and Myth."

For *Ulysses* portended a possible end to "narrative method," or an alternative at any rate. Before the paragraph quoted, Eliot announced that the novel was finished as a form; indeed it had not been a form, but "the expression of an age which had not sufficiently lost all form to feel the need of something stricter." The present age with its "futility and anarchy" would need form, order, significance in its art at least; and for this it might look to "the mythical method." This being his line of reasoning, it is clear why he viewed Joyce's parallel to the *Odyssey* as important. It was in his terms a "classical" device; that is a means of dealing artistically with, as he said, "living material." The conception of myth as imposing an order upon modern life repeats his demand for an "important" and "coherent" point of view in art in the *Tyro* articles of 1921. The "mythical method" was his own, whatever it meant for *Ulysses*. Conditioned by psychology, ethnology and Frazer's *The Golden Bough*, it was specifically the method of *The Waste Land*. A. Walton Litz observed some years ago in his essay "*The Waste Land* Fifty Years After" (1972) that the use of the Grail legend by the one was not analogous to the use of the *Odyssey* by the other. I agree in this measure: the *Odyssey* for Joyce controlled a complex narrative, but the Grail legend for Eliot formed a single element, though even so the most significant one, in a presentation of scenes. Yet this presentation, too, relates a series of events; it may correctly be termed an oblique narrative, being Tiresias' review of his time and of the times gathered into his time. Instead of chronicling, it evokes dramatic moments of consciousness and self-consciousness; and instead of projecting these cinemato-graphically in detachment from Tiresias, it reenacts them in his mind. No one of the traditional myths, not even the Grail legend, satisfies the requirements laid upon the mythical method by Eliot; it is when all are taken together that they mould a shape and compose a disguise to objectify experience for the poet, and in changing this into a world of feeling conditioned by themselves, may be said to "order" the contemporary panorama. First they report the painful history of a life that becomes a myth as it creates its own labyrinth, but by doing so they expose a significance beyond this. The method suggests that through myth art may express a sense of the present; but it must be remembered that the artist's point of view is personal, not social. However social the world of Eliot's myth, however faithfully an image of that "immense panorama," its imaginative roots reach to a personal level unexposed in the review of *Ulysses*.

"Ulysses, Order, and Myth" has not been approached quizzi-cally enough. One may come away from it in doubt whether Eliot thought *Ulysses* "narrative" or "mythical" or both. His backing and filling with the notion of the novel as form yet not form, and with the relation of *Ulysses* to the novel; his shift of focus from "form," which controls a book, to "method," which as described controls "contemporary history" in Joyce's book—these are typical and dis-couraging manifestations of unwillingness to be pinned down. When Eliot's demonstration seems loose it is really tight; but to criticise it meticulously would not in this case reveal whether certain possible inferences from the review are necessary implications of it. One inference, that the mythical method supersedes the narrative, is defied by *Ulysses*; this is too suggestive to neglect, for its implication may be that Eliot was reserving his enthusiasm for something else. Per-haps *Ulysses*, after all, balked the ideal.

The date, it must be recalled, was November 1923. The mythical method that swept narrative into the past (so bad was Eliot's proph-ecy) was being perfected in Joyce's work in progress, the future *Finnegans Wake* (1939). *Ulysses* once published, Joyce had laid plans for this masterpiece in 1922; and though according to his biographer

Richard Ellmann he progressed slowly, he was in time to greet the vernal equinox of 1923 with a few pages of text which he augmented in the course of the year. Eliot's review, solicited, was friendly in tone and directed attention to Joyce's use of myth; that sufficed for the moment. Eliot had followed all the fortunes of *Ulysses*, reading the serialised parts and then, in manuscript, the later ones. In 1920 he had cycled to Paris with Wyndham Lewis to meet Joyce, whose stupendous work lay unfinished; it is likely that he read some of it, perhaps drafts of "Circe," on the spot. By mid-1921 he had read it all. Pound (who after its official completion in October 1921 declared the Christian Era at an end and drew up a new calendar to inaugurate the age "P.S.U."—"after the writing of *Ulysses*") had Eliot's ear all this time and kept him informed about Joyce's purposes in so far as disclosed. Eliot, possibly as a result of *Ulysses*, conceived that a point of view was "myth," a vision significantly projected as an enduring new image in art. From *Ulysses* he borrowed for "Gerontion" the device of interacting levels of time and in *The Waste Land* used it again for his palimpsest; but unlike Joyce, who always kept the past distinct from the present, he *blended* the levels in a manner suggestive of Pound, later, in the *Cantos*. Also he lifted for *The Waste Land* (as I was the first to point out, 1950) a few images which likewise he handled differently from Joyce. There is no probability that he derived his structural device, the spectator–unifier, from the monologuists in *Ulysses*. His critical use of the Grail legend differs from Joyce's mechanical use of the *Odyssey*. Eliot said that the *Odyssey* parallel had "the importance of a scientific discovery"; this was astute, for Joyce used it like a rigid formula for the classification of his episodes. At the same time it may well have been Joyce's work that furnished to Eliot's the idea of myth, in which case, even if Eliot was the inventor of the method he described, Joyce was its begetter.

Here is a certain relation, that of two works one of which affected the other; but the two differed extremely in method. Yet, given the opportunity of commenting on the method of *Ulysses*, Eliot substituted the definition of quite another procedure, which accomplished narrative but did not narrate. There was, one now sees, an absolute discrepancy between Joyce's "parallel use of the Odyssey" and the "continuous parallel between contemporaneity and antiquity" in Eliot's mythic vision. The one was a mode of structuring a representation, of ordering the relation of the actors in a probable narrative. The other, Eliot's, was a mode of transforming and pre-

senting, of displaying a psychological dimension as a mythic landscape. Joyce's *Ulysses* has indeed been analysed to yield up psychological archetypes. Its whole mythic apparatus nevertheless remains
ancillary; it is myth used, not created; used formally, decoratively,
as an inflated exhibition of wit. By describing in his review a mythical
method that pertained to something else, Eliot sidestepped a due
acknowledgement of Joyce's art as a novelist. This novel had done
what the novel can best do—create a moral vision like the one Eliot
saw in Baudelaire. Joyce—in the words of Eliot in the *Dial* of August
1921—had made "an articulate external world." It may be that the
coherent world of *Ulysses* composed too exceptional a "myth" altogether; that the Blooms and Stephen Dedalus and their vivid world
were too real for Eliot, too true to behaviour and too likely to prove
immortal.

Joyce had various schemes for partitioning and structuring *Ulysses*; they reveal that, however the grouping of the chapters might
have differed, his anxiety for a formal pattern led him to allegorical
rather than mythical effects. His Renaissance imagination gave birth
to microcosmic figures. For example the book *Ulysses*, like the House
of Temperance in Spenser, is the body of a man, archetypal Man;
and it is composed, chapter by chapter, of organs. These are arranged
in a hierarchy: first three organs for Aristotle's rational soul, consisting of the Augustinian parts of the mind, Will, Memory, Understanding; then twelve organs for Aristotle's appetitive soul; then
three more for Aristotle's vegetative soul. Other sets of correspondences coexist easily with these, including the parallel to the *Odyssey*
and the *Argonautica*. Internally this creature, like a macrocosm, contains microcosmic small creatures or homunculi who relate to one
another according to still other figures; that is, the several characters
of the novel form among themselves emblematic or logical patterns.
As one of Eliot's 1922 comments on the book points out, burlesque
abounds ("London Letter," *Dial*, vol. 73). No Protestant divine of
the old school, learned in the book of Revelation, would have failed
to identify the Woman whose number is Seven and whose seat is
Eccles Street—a pun on the Latin for "Church" provided happily by
the map of Dublin. The essential meaninglessness of such a design
to the actual life spread out for the reader of *Ulysses* testifies to the
power of Joyce's realism. It is as if the dozens of correspondences
were present to characterise the Dublin world's indifference to them,
and so to characterise it. The Renaissance devices perform the task

not of enriching the present but of isolating it historically. Instead of Eliot's "continuous parallel between contemporaneity and antiquity" (a phrase which ill describes the *Odyssey* parallel) there are a *present* in microscopic exposure and a *past* blurred and out of focus. Concerning the *Odyssey* as such, *Ulysses* says nothing whatever; for, in contrast with Eliot, who refused to see the present except through the past, Joyce was hardly interested in the past at all.

In *Ulysses* Joyce's structural use of prior myth shows the modern world in an unmythological light; the end of Eliot's is to transform all into myth. Joyce's method resembles travesty; Eliot's, mock-epic. The principle of the mythical method inheres in *The Rape of the Lock*, though Pope does not account for all that Eliot did with mythic parallels. The essential is a technique forcing the myth to criticise the modern world, which furthermore *The Waste Land* uses to modify the reader's idea of traditional myth, in conformity with "Tradition and the Individual Talent." The ancient and modern fuse into a new image. Eliot's ironical and patronising nod to his superior, Yeats, in "Ulysses, Order, and Myth" ("the horoscope is auspicious") paid indeed a tribute to a better craftsman of myth. Yeats did not welcome Joyce's and Eliot's competition, but that is another story. Reciprocity of criticism between myth and modernity abounds in Yeats and acts like circuitry for his system. Thus in a poem written when the system was emergent, "No Second Troy." Here any number of Helens—Dryden's new Helen in "Alexander's Feast" (who "fired another Troy"), Homer's, Euripides', Marlowe's, Goethe's—combine in an image both to glorify and to rebuke Yeats's Helen of the contemporary age. No less, the modern Helen by her unconscionable fanaticism and violence of intent makes over the image of the legendary Helen, who is still what the intervening poets have depicted but changed by this addition. Here myth is both used and created, and the two processes are made one. The splendour of Yeats's method resides in its tragic irony, to which Joyce and Eliot cannot rise.

Reflecting on *Ulysses* but looking beyond it to his own synthesis in *The Waste Land*, Eliot contrived in "Ulysses, Order, and Myth" a recipe for literature which should transcend narrative and incorporate the hypotheses of the social sciences, and such discoveries as those marshalled in Frazer's *The Golden Bough*. These had in common a revelation of the primitive, the savage and unconscious; they fathomed the regions from which myth arose, the impulses that gave rise to ritual, and the processes in premodern minds that erupted in modern minds as poetry. Their intimation of a continuity in the human psyche, a prolongation of remote and forgotten rhythms, could supply both the matter and the model for art. Eliot's obsessive theme was the persistence of the past; artistic technique could demonstrate that in modern culture all ages mingle; already *The Waste Land* had produced a multilayered mixture of allusions and literary thefts. In such a construct every detail can implicitly criticise by its bare presence all comparable details. No detail is meaningful alone. Eliot seems not to have liked *Ulysses* so much as he admired it; it is questionable whether he detected in it as much artistic merit as in the method he was praising. It may be that he wanted his readers to remember the mythic concentration in *The Waste Land*. Perhaps he himself associated the mythic mixture not only with his poem but with the bruited new experiment of Joyce: "Mr Joyce is pursuing a method . . . " In the work in progress to which Joyce would dedicate the labour of two decades, *Finnegans Wake*, narrative would be attenuated to the vanishing point; an interminable spiralling parallel of all times, past and future, would return upon itself in a bewildering scheme predicated as the eternal present of an all-embracing consciousness, which nevertheless is an unconscious mind; and in this mind and containing personality, the spectator of all, all individualities would be united. This whirlpool appears in the finished book as, except in its linguistic evolutions, an enormously magnified variation on the mythic plan of *The Waste Land*.

When Joyce and Eliot were lads, the authorities in the United States arrested and convicted the remarkable freehand counterfeiter Jim the Penman; his real name was Emmanuel Ninger. This artist, whose impeccably drawn pen-and-ink replicas of fifty-dollar bills readily passed as genuine, lived modestly, forging notes one at a time as needed. He was found out in 1896 when a fresh example of his skill, its ink perhaps not quite dry, was laid down on a wet bar. Slurring his name to Shem the Penman, Joyce in *Finnegans Wake* adopted him as, among various avatars, a type of the literary artist, and twinned him with an opposite, Shaun the Postman, who at one juncture in their immemorial warfare manifests his own mercenary appreciation of art by allegedly stealing Shem the Penman's manuscript. It is accepted that this relationship and especially this incident refer to Joyce's belief that Eliot stole the substance of *The Waste Land* from *Ulysses*. But did Joyce steal the mythic structure of *Finnegans Wake* from *The Waste Land*? And was Eliot privately laying claim to it in "Ulysses, Order, and Myth"? Certain strategies of Eliot's poem may be seen in *Ulysses*, but scattered about in it. In *Finnegans Wake* they are combined with one another, as in Tiresias and his layered times. Eliot's "Notes" to *The Waste Land* were written in the summer of 1922, and between then and the end of the year Joyce was maturing his scheme for a myth to take in everything. One thing is certain: Eliot's moral vision was his own and Joyce was invincibly indifferent to it as he pursued an experiment with language that no one could steal. The psychology of one forger poses ethical problems; that of two watching each other operate and coveting each other's papers provokes the disinterested laughter of scholarship. . . .

The composition of the first draft of "The Fire Sermon," with which *The Waste Land* began, attended two literary experiences—among many others. One of these, as Kenner signalised, was Eliot's reading of *John Dryden: A Study of His Poetry* by Mark Van Doren. There is proof of this link apart from Kenner's hypothesis. The other experience, also documented and circumstantially relevant, was Eliot's *bouleversement* by the "Circe" chapter of *Ulysses*, which he read in manuscript and applauded in a letter to Joyce on 21 May 1921 (quoted in Day, 1971). If these readings jointly affected "The Fire Sermon," they did so by bringing Tiresias into it and by shaping Eliot's representation of his traditional aspect. . . . There is little doubt about the timing at least. Eliot's statement of 9 May that his poem was "partly on paper" accompanied the information that he had been reading "the latter part of Ulysses" (*Facsimile*). He probably wrote the *John Dryden* review in May, for it was published on 9 June (*The Times Literary Supplement*, no. 1012). It is my hypothesis that Tiresias was introduced into the poem in May, and that his presence was owing, among other factors, to Eliot's reading of Van Doren and Joyce. Tiresias' function as central intelligence derived from the novel, from Conrad and James notably (see Litz, 1973); but his mythic role had various prototypes—indeed almost too many.

Discovering the Corpus

Gregory S. Jay

Then I—I shall begin again. I shall not cease until I bring the truth to light. Apollo has shown, and you have shown, the duty which we owe the dead. You have my gratitude. You will find me a firm ally, and together we shall exact vengeance for our land and for the god. I shall not rest till I dispel this defilement—not just for another man's sake, but for my own as well. For whoever the assassin—he might turn his hand against me too. Yes, I shall be serving Laius and myself.

Oedipus Tyrannus

The detective and the literary critic are often compared. Each undertakes to solve a mystery, working from scattered clues to piece together the meaning of disparate events. This is a hermeneutic quest, as the detective-critic discloses at last the surprising truths behind apparently random appearances. Ideally, a "totalization" or systematic comprehension of fragments is the result. The figure of the sleuth appeals to every reader's desire to detect a pattern in life's haphazard flow of things; our interest is more intensely fixed when there has been a crime, since the violation of the law stands metaphorically for the negation of meaning in general, for an outbreak of transgression that threatens to bring down the orders of significance established by the law's logos. So it is that many critics take special interest

From *T. S. Eliot and the Poetics of Literary History*. © 1983 by Louisiana State University Press.

(at least of late) in texts that disobey laws, genres, or conventions. Theoretical critics tend to pursue these literary felonies after the formal or aesthetic case is closed, inquiring at the doors of philosophy, linguistics, psychoanalysis, and history, and throughout the neighborhood of the human sciences for the agents of disharmony.

But who has been slain in *The Waste Land*? The intrigue deepens when we realize that the victim, the assailant, and the detective are interchangeable metaphors. The predicament of Oedipus dramatizes this tragic condensation of roles, the entanglements of which will preoccupy much of Eliot's poem. We have seen [elsewhere] the similar case of the Quester and the Fisher King. The disturbing indistinction between, or identification of, Oedipus and Laius or Quester and King repeats the "peculiar personal intimacy" of poetic sons and fathers. The addition of the detective (a vocation thrust upon both Oedipus and the Quester) to this relation figures the desire to resolve its paradoxes and to reinstitute the power of the law. The poem enacts this effort to unravel the mystery and restore order. Yet simultaneously, in form and conception, it compulsively repeats the crime, transgresses the inherited rules of writing, and dismembers the unity of the fathers' words. Adding another turn of the screw, the poem presents this fragmentation of truth as the death of the speaker or author himself. We are asked to mourn his life as well, though self-murder is the planned escape from "personality" back to the soul's eternal life. The stylistic subordination of personal voice to borrowings, echoes, and allusions performs an askesis that violates the unity of self and tradition. "What happens" to the poet, wrote Eliot in 1919, "is a continual surrender of himself as he is at the moment to something which is more valuable. The progress of an artist is a continual self-sacrifice, a continual extinction of personality." The body of tradition and the poet himself suffer willingly, or by the will of the poet, the ritual of the *sparagmos*. This is part of the relevance of the vegetation god ceremonies, as they too dramatize an identification of the god with the life of the people who recurrently slay him in the name of fertility. The god's resurrection and the nation's rejuvenation culminate another restricted economy of the *Aufhebung*, in which castration and death are the *via negativa* of potency and life. As I will argue later, this pattern informs *The Waste Land*'s modernist revision of the pastoral elegy, the genre whose laws the poem subjects to uncanny interpretations.

It would be nothing new simply to observe that *The Waste Land* violates literary (and other) laws or that like many such texts it places the reader quite self-consciously in the occupation of the hermeneutic detective. The criminal themes of murder and adultery serve this function and provide self-consuming models for the resolution of the poem as a whole. An avid fan of Conan Doyle and founding member of a Sherlock Holmes fan club, Eliot presents us with a puzzling array of remains that increase our suspicion that a coherent, though horror-filled, story lies behind the "heap of broken images." Dead men turn up everywhere in this unreal city, or their words float to its allusive surface. The story begins like a good melodrama at the victim's burial service and proceeds in disjointed flashbacks to piece together the tale of his loves and losses. But the victim is protean, as are his assailants, and hermaphrodite and polysemous. The corpse's casket is a library, his obituary everyman's. The poem's criminal atmosphere filches much of its scenery from Eliot's reading of Shakespearean and Jacobean tragedy, through numerous allusions to adultery and murder in Webster, Middleton, and others. Eliot's voyeuristic involvement with the sordid had also prompted his earlier verse on urban horrors, his taste for Baudelaire and for *Bubu of Montparnasse*, the story of a Parisian whore for which he wrote a preface. He was fascinated by that English tradition of popular tabloid gossip about the criminal, which seemed to be a modern Jacobean-ism. With similar motives Eliot consistently ranks Poe, elegist of dead beauties and inventor of detective fictions, among the three or four American writers worthy of his attention.

The poem's origin in this tradition of low crime, sordid mystery, and dark artistry is evidenced in the manuscripts, where the original title, "He Do the Police in Different Voices," is taken from Dickens's *Our Mutual Friend*. In the passage Eliot has in mind, Sloppy performs a kind of ventriloquism as he reads the newspaper text that tells of ghastly doings, providing an obvious source for *The Waste Land*'s polyvocal method. *Our Mutual Friend* contains not only a model for Eliot's revoicings, but a protagonist come back from the dead. John Harmon rises from the waters of the Thames to inhabit London in the disguise of John Rokesmith, covertly observing the fate of his own entailed inheritance, concretely symbolized by the mounds of waste that are the novel's thematic and ironic narrative centers. In erasing his own identity, Harmon, like the Duke in Shakespeare's *Measure for Measure*, compounds and perpetuates the disharmony of his realm. Eliot may also have been thinking of Dickens's *Bleak*

House, whose Detective Bucket is one of the first great English comic sleuths. That novel, as J. Hillis Miller has written, brilliantly examines the problems of wills, testaments, and legacies lost in a hopeless mire of documents and interpretations disputed interminably. The novel's characters find themselves bewildered by a mountain of wastepaper. Esther Hawdon, one of the novel's two narrators, tells her tale in an effort to uncover, detective fashion, the truth of her own parentage. Her mother, Lady Dedlock, is an "exhausted deity," an artist of deceptive self-representation. Her dead father, the shadowy Captain Hawdon, was, we are not surprised to learn, a legal copyist—a textual nobody like Melville's Bartleby. His death parallels in implication the farcical court case of Jarndyce and Jarndyce: both represent the breakdown of lawful, authoritative, ordered scripts. The revelations of the novel lead in the end to Esther's marriage and the construction of another Bleak House, an edifice not unlike Dickens's book, which problematically hopes to restore what has been wasted. Eliot agreed that it was Dickens's "best novel" and "finest piece of construction."

The motifs of detection, scattered writings, adulteries, and sacred mysteries may be traced in a second deleted title. Part 2, "A Game of Chess," first bore the designation "In the Cage," the title of Henry James's tale of a young woman whose job in a telegraph-office cage makes her privy to the cryptic secrets of high-society lovers. Valerie Eliot ascribes this title instead to the passage from Petronius that provided Eliot with his epigraph of the Cumaen sibyl. Grover Smith concludes that this explanation "does not hold up," though he declares that James's story "has no particular relevance to Part II of the poem." On the contrary, it strikingly prefigures Eliot's formal and thematic concerns. James uses the figure of the sibyl ironically in his portrait of the girl whose function is "to dole out stamps and postal orders, weigh letters, answer stupid questions, give difficult change and, more than anything else, count words as numberless as the sands of time." She occupies a vortex of writings, exercising her "instinct of observation and detection" in guessing "the high reality, the bristling truth" of the fragmentary messages that pass before her. Although she "was perfectly aware that her imaginative life was the life in which she spent most of her time," supplemented by "greasy" novels "all about fine folks," the girl scarcely perceives the disparity between her projections of sublime Romantic love and the seedier reality of her clients' adulterous liaisons. She finds her ladies and gentlemen "always in communication," and "she read into the immensity of their intercourse stories and meanings without end." Her folly in so mistaking her own wish fulfillment—that Romantic love might sweep her transcendentally out of the plebeian world of her intended Mr. Mudge and into the aristocratic sublime—informs Eliot's placement before his readers of the cryptic evidence of so many sordid or tragic liaisons contemporary and antique. James's tale illustrates a point Eliot would insist upon, that Romanticism looks to relations in this world for a Truth that lies beyond it. James's social point—that her sublime is a trick that cheap romantic novels play on the hearts of the lower class—becomes in Eliot the conviction that he has been seduced by his precursors' imaginative achievement of an erotic union of the mind with the world it reads.

The girl in the cage concentrates her powers upon a single case, that of the adulterous communication between Lady Bradeen and Captain Everard. (James was shameless in his names!) Like the chess game's king, Everard is the weakest player in James's complicated love game: "he only fidgeted and floundered in his want of power." In this society, like that of *The Waste Land*, "it was much more the women, on the whole, who were after the men than the men who were after the women." Perhaps it was this underscoring of the castration thematic so recurrent in James that led Eliot to decoy his readers with a change of title. Moreover, the figure of the girl as sibyl and decoder would have been assimilated to that of Eliot himself, identifying her Romanticism as the cause of interpretative impotence, since in the end she gets it all quite muddled: "what our heroine saw and felt for in the whole business was the vivid reflexion of her own dreams and delusions and her own return to reality." This acceptance of the reality principle represents the girl's askesis. Her biological femininity does not preclude, but underlies, her participation in a castration psychology that has shaped her search for the missing truth from the start.

James's tale links Eros, truth, writing, and the phallus in the girl's pursuit of Everard's mystery. "It came to her there, with her eyes on his face, that she held the whole thing in her hand, held it as she held her pencil, which might have broken at that instant in her tightened grip. This made her feel like the fountain of fate." Poor Everard! When she grasps the "truth" of his letters and affairs, she purloins the phallus and restores it to her own incomplete self. In this she, as much as any of James's bachelor epistemologists, figures the Romantic author as castrated/castrating in the quest for a condensed logos of sex, writing, and knowledge. At the end, however, she learns that her salvation of Everard through recollection of the lovers' letters only dooms him to Lady Bradeen's clutches. In the economy of phallogocentrism, the truth of the letter always requires the dispossession of its former owner: the girl has unwittingly emasculated Everard in knowing him. The truth she is left with is the "truth" of his castration, as we are left with the uncanny notion that "truth" in writing "castrates" life. Renouncing her sibyl's job and marrying Mr. Mudge, the girl gives up the Romantic and phallogocentric vocations for a less metaphysical career. Eliot's poem takes up her career once more in deciphering the logos of scattered parts. It restages the drama of James's tale, expressing once more the Romantic longing to find Truth through the incarnations of Eros, discovering once more that the truth of sexuality is loss, difference, and the adulteration of identity. In its negative theology, *The Waste Land* repeatedly returns to castration as truth, subl(im)ating the deconstruction of Romantic Eros into another quest for the divine love that can fulfill the desires human life seems to imitate with its carnal appetites. The fragmentation of truth in the poem operates, according to such logic, to spur our critical desire to locate and regenerate what has been lost, and it represses, by its very hyperbole and lamentation, the prerequisite of castration as the "original" scene of the crime. Only in aspects of its conclusion does the poem come round to a reconciliation with the dissemination of the father's word.

Correspondences with James's tale shed light on at least the first two parts of "A Game of Chess," with its evocations of insufferable women, male fear, and marital discord. At the heart of these mournful mysteries lies the retelling of paradise lost. As his footnote tells us, Eliot borrows his "sylvan scene" from Milton (and, quite tellingly behind that, from Spenser's accounts of Venus and Adonis and of the Bower of Bliss) for his own revisionary display of "The change of Philomel, by the barbarous king/ So rudely forced." She becomes the genius loci of a "romantic" transmutation of loss into a redemptive, artful song. What Eliot adds to our hearing, literally so in the manuscript, is "lust," the unsublimated drive that violates the virgin garden of woman and man's identity. The element of incest in the rape of Philomel by Tereus may appear irrelevant here unless we understand desire's threat to kinship systems and thus by exten-

sion to the structuring of a stable and meaningful economy of differences. Philomel represents woman as an object of prohibited
desire, and we are left wondering whether that prohibition originates
in genealogy (in which case she would be a metaphor of the mother)
or in a "classical" deconstruction of a "romantic" metaphysics of art
and Eros.

These complex associations may be further detected, if not resolved, by reference to a clue overheard by that exceptional aural
sleuth, John Hollander. He notices that the second reference to Philomel's song, in "The Fire Sermon," reads "So rudely forc'd," and
he argues that "there is nothing to explain the peculiar spelling 'forc'd'
at this point, except a Miltonic echo," from "Lycidas": "And with
forc'd fingers rude." What correlation can there be, beyond the general "milieu of the drowned poet," between the king's rape of Philomel and Milton's untimely plucking of the berries? The answer, I
think, lies in the elegiac strategy of poetic resurrection intrinsic to
Milton's transumption of the genre in "Lycidas," that is, in his rebirth
as a poet after this "violation" of Mother Nature and the Muse.
Milton's "inviolable voice" haunts new poets with its power to create
a highly individual beauty out of its "Babylonish" troping of the
language and inheritance. Eliot's king is called "barbarous," meaning
he literally speaks an unacceptable language, an eccentric tongue.
The speaker of "Lycidas" presumes to grasp the laurel crown before
his time, pressured into it, he says, by the death of Edward King.
To tradition he says he must "Shatter your leaves before the mel-
lowing year," where "Shatter" connotes not only the traditional
ritual scattering of leaves but a destructive shattering as well. The
song of Philomel, then, once more inscribes the poet's ambivalence
toward beginning again his attempt upon the sublime and condenses
the problems involved with those of sexuality. Thus, the passage
expresses 1) a fear of the father-precursor's prohibition, 2) a desire
to scatter the words of the father by violating his Muse, 3) a dread
that he may not have the power to regather the leaves in a new
volume of love, and 4) a transfiguring urge to reject the whole "romantic" problematic as delusory compared to a complete askesis and
retheologization of desires poetic and sexual.

The section had opened, in fact, with a revision of a precursor.
Eliot twists Shakespeare's lines on Cleopatra into an elegantly suf-
focating portrait of the lady, thus contradicting all his warnings about
Shakespeare's bad influence in the sense that his defensive parody

both confirms Shakespeare's stylistic preeminence in its absence and improves upon it with additions from other dead masters. Frequently cited in Eliot's criticism, *Antony and Cleopatra* holds a high station in his canon. The play's theme of a hero led astray by his infatuation with a beautiful woman illustrates one of Eliot's key obsessions, vacillating as it does between adoration and condemnation. He had given the lines "she looks like sleep, / As she would catch another Antony / In her strong toil of grace" as an example of Shakespeare's "complicated" metaphors, remarking that the trope's additive quality was "a reminder of that fascination of Cleopatra which shaped her history and that of the world, and of that fascination being so strong that it prevails even in death." The fascination of Cleopatra stands for the fascination of Shakespearean metaphor: both exceed, add, tempt one beyond confirmed identity, whereas Dante's "visual" metaphors reveal truth. Cleopatra seduces as Shakespeare's poetic style can seduce, turning her victims into predecessors of James's deluded romantic girl. Antony's fate echoes Captain Everard's, while Enobarbus is made into yet another blinded prophet. Sifting through Shakespeare's leaves, Eliot is lured but suspicious, and he mocks the folly of Enobarbus and of misreaders who have failed to hear Shakespeare's irony as he dramatically presents yet another victim of Cleopatra's self-representations. Revising Shakespeare's style, Eliot overloads the imagery of his lines to create a dissociation of sensibility. He compounds the Jacobeans, the eighteenth-century baroque, and fin de siècle aestheticism in a hyperbolic illustration of the snares of sensual imaginings. He brings to the surface the purport of Shakespeare's speech with the aid of its setting in his own poem, among the fearful females, deluded men, and parodied styles.

The failure of romanticism to find in human experiences the sublime it projects as lost also pervades the disharmony of the nervous couple in the subsequent lines of "A Game of Chess." As the opening section dwelled upon the femme fatale, this conversation, or lack of one, indicates the concurrent absence of the saving woman who provides access to life, creation, presence, and the Absolute. While "nothing" occurs between these two, all the action takes place off-stage. The section's title and Eliot's note refer us to Middleton's *Women Beware Women* and Bianca's forced seduction, which occurs while her mother-in-law is distracted by a chess game with the procuress. "The wind under the door" sends us to Webster's *The Devil's Law Case*, in which it brings news of a man's wounding. Another primal scene, then, of woman's violation and man's vital loss takes place within earshot of this couple and within an imagistic and allusive context of reiterated blindness. It was also, Grover Smith notes, "with a noise and shaking, and with a blast of wind, that the dead in Ezekiel's valley of dry bones received the breath of life and stood upon their feet." In the manuscript, what the wind was doing was "Carrying / Away the little light dead people," a theft from the Paolo and Francesca episode in *Inferno*, canto 5. Of them Eliot wrote: "To have lost all recollected delight would have been, for Francesca, either loss of humanity or relief from damnation. The ecstasy, with the present thrill at the remembrance of it, is a part of the torture. Francesca is neither stupefied nor reformed; she is merely damned; and it is part of damnation to experience desires that we can no longer gratify." The speaker in Eliot's poem either cannot gratify his desires or gratifies them at the cost of a greater damnation. Eliot's couple, in Dantean fashion, seem eternally damned to the condition of unsatisfied longing. Intercourse of any kind appears impossible in this "rat's alley / Where the dead men lost their bones."

What obstacle prevents speech, thought, or action here? The "loss" of "bones" imaged in the man's words voices a connection between present impotence and past losses or glories. He is hardly present at all, in fact, as his mind is usurped by repetitive memories that possess him. The significance of this haunting may be seen in a look at Eliot's revisions. The printed draft reads, "I remember / Those are pearls that were his eyes." The manuscript reads: "I remember / The hyacinth garden. Those are pearls that were his eyes, yes!" Pound left these lines unaltered, except to suggest cutting the allusion to Molly's soliloquy in *Ulysses* (a relevant tale of adulteries and wandering paternities). Vivienne Eliot inexplicably penned "Yes & wonderful wonderful" in the margin. The decision to drop this reference to the hyacinth garden was evidently Eliot's own. Perhaps he felt that having his speaker recall that former ecstasy here would be too obvious an irony. He may also have been uncomfortable with the conjunction of a lover's tryst with a father's death or of the loss of love and the loss of eyes. Some have even argued that the excision covers up a reference to Jean Verdenal and Eliot's attraction to him, a sensational and untenable speculation. A more viable biographical reading would be that the passage implies that the man's memory of a former love makes his disillusionment with a present wife crippling and that Eliot would not have thrown such a message at Vivienne in public, whatever her perception of the lines' import. He was too caring and solicitous toward her feelings for that, even if the lines were simply intended to express impersonally the difference between an ideal regenerative love and a spiritless communication. The juxtaposition of hyacinth garden and Ariel's song would have been helpful, however, in pointing out the links between these two scenes of love, loss, and metamorphosis. They emerge from a "romantic" desire for translation into a beatified state, transfiguring loss into pearls as precious as Molly's final, loving affirmation of her moment as Bloom's flower of the mountain. Incoherence plagues the speaker of the scene because, by measure of past or figurally constructed images, his emotions cannot find any available or adequate object. A poetic coherence, however, holds these lines and themes and allusions in a paratactic assemblage that puts the techniques of imagism and symbolism to their best use: a vital tension stays suspended between the incoherence of the represented and the skill with which Eliot draws us on to read his articulations of its origins and ends as we play sibyl to the poem's leaves.

The foregoing investigations of a few intertextual case histories in *The Waste Land* demonstrate how quickly the poem eludes interpretative or aesthetic closure. At the risk of scattering an already shattering poem, these forays seemed strategically prerequisite to theoretical questions about how to read or name this text, since criticism and canon formation have already so tamed its uncanniness for us. It might be healthy to restore our sense of how aberrant the poem is, as any undergraduate would gladly tell us.

Reviewing Eliot's experiment after its initial publication, Louis Untermeyer wrote, "It is doubtful whether 'The Waste Land' is anything but a set of separate poems, a piece of literary carpentry, a scholarly joiner's work, the flotsam and jetsam of dessicated culture," or simply a "pompous parade of erudition." These are pertinent insights, though not in the derogatory sense that Untermeyer intends. Inspection of the published manuscripts now confirms that Eliot did indeed assemble his poem from myriad jottings, some nearly ten years in the keeping. Most of the poem as we have it was set down in 1921 and 1922, undergoing a famous series of revisions at the hands of Eliot, his wife, and Ezra Pound. At the literal level this history exhibits processes ordinarily disguised in the presentation of supposedly unitary, orderly texts ascribable to a single authorial consciousness. Untermeyer's critical a priori posits the existence and

privilege of a metaphysically conceived writing, set down instanta-
neously and forever by a voice speaking an isolable truth. This formalist object would above all things be "separate," individually
differentiated, whole, and free of the past. Eliot's "poem," however,
is an intertextual phenomenon, conspicuously a process of allusive
appropriation. *The Waste Land* demonstrates Eliot's theory of tradition and Harold Bloom's insistence on intertextuality. There are
no individual, self-contained poems. The "poem" lies in the relations
between poems, in the troping of an ancestor. Has Eliot allowed us
to say who "wrote" *The Waste Land*? What do we think we mean
if we say that Eliot wrote:

> Frisch weht der Wind
> Der Heimat zu.
> Mein Irisch Kind,
> Wo weilest du?

These lines from Wagner were the German's property, but their
properties are in Eliot's hands now.

Untermeyer's metaphors for the poem ("literary carpentry, a
scholarly joiner's work") point again to Lévi-Strauss's notion of *bricolage* and to an idea of poetry as the opportune arrangement of
whatever happens to be at hand rather than as the mimesis of an
organic or transcendent architecture. Yet, before endorsing *bricolage*
as a master metaphor of the text, we should recall [Jacques] Derrida's
argument that "if the difference between *bricoleur* and engineer is
basically theological, the very concept of *bricolage* implies a fall and
an accidental finitude." *Bricolage*, like belatedness and other mythologies of lost Golden Ages, retrospectively invests an absent figure
with the status of an Origin. Ironically, the bricoleur's technique in
The Waste Land rebuilds, albeit through lament and eulogy, the value
of metaliterary and metaphysical constructs that writing might mirror rather than piece together: "What are the roots that clutch, what
branches grow / Out of this stony rubbish?" The possibility of an
organic logos springing up out of all this textual rubbish is suggested
by the figural language here, but in its contextual allusion to the
resurrection of the bones in Ezekiel the passage looks instead to a
transcendent power for salvation. The use of *bricolage*, or the allusive
method, in *The Waste Land* does transgress the conventions of poetry,
but like any transgression it simultaneously re-marks the place of the
law.

Bricolage and engineering, like the artificial and the organic or the chaotic and the orderly, fall into a binary opposition of the kind that Hegel puts to work in the following relevant passage.

> The encyclopaedia of philosophy must not be confounded with ordinary encyclopaedias. An ordinary encyclopaedia does not pretend to be more than an aggregation of sciences, regulated by no principle, and merely as experience offers them. Sometimes it even includes what merely bear the name of sciences, while they are nothing more than a collection of bits of information. In an aggregate like this, the several branches of knowledge owe their place in the encyclopaedia to extrinsic reasons, and their unity is therefore artificial: they are *arranged*, but we cannot say that they form a *system*. For the same reason, especially as the materials to be combined also depend upon no one rule or principle, the arrangment is at best an experiment, and will always exhibit inequalities.

The distinction between the "ordinary encyclopaedia" and the "encyclopaedia of philosophy" seems to parallel the one between the nineteenth-century poem of organic unity and the twentieth-century poem of fragments. "On Margate Sands / I can connect / Nothing with nothing." How many readers of *The Waste Land* or Pound's *Cantos* have come away thinking that "they are *arranged*, but we cannot say that they form a *system*"? This is not quite the case, however, as with Eliot we have any number of systems alluded to as possible keys—myth, anthropology, mysticism, religion, the tarot, and even literary criticism. The poem experiments with these systems of interpretation by inviting the detective-critic to try them out on the aggregation of entries stolen from other encyclopedias. Eliot's famous dictum bears repeating: "The good poet welds his theft into a whole of feeling which is unique, utterly different from that from which it was torn; the bad throws it into something which has no cohesion." "Torn" implicitly plays upon the metaphor of the dismembered body, utilizing the traditional aesthetic description of a work as "shapely" or "monstrous," as in the opening of Horace's *Ars Poetica*. Only if the purloined goods are re-membered in a coherent new body, "whole" and "unique," is theft pardonable.

What is this "cohesion?" In contrast to Hegel's "system," Eliot gives us an emotion rather than an epistemology. "I cannot make it cohere," wrote Pound in Canto 116, after a lifetime's work at a poem that, one could argue, never strayed from the method Eliot advanced and then abandoned in *The Waste Land*. Cohesion stems from the Latin *haerere*, to stick together. Its cognates include adherence, adhesion, and hesitation. The principle of connection in each is paratactic: discontinuous elements are held together but not integrally so, their relations being not so much of interiors coordinated as of exteriors juxtaposed in tension or suspension. This sticking may also lead to hesitation, an occupation of the adherent ground between oppositions. In fact, in "Prufrock" and *The Waste Land*, it is this condition of hesitation that is the "whole of feeling." In a letter to Richard Aldington on the eve of his journey to Margate, Lausanne, and the completion of the poem, Eliot writes, "I am satisfied, since being here, that my 'nerves' are a very mild affair, due not to overwork but to an aboulie and emotional derangement which has been a lifelong affliction. Nothing wrong with my mind." *Aboulie* is a variant of *abulia*, a psychiatric term for the loss or impairment of the ability to decide or act independently. This emotional state pervades and unites the poem, though ironically, for it is a unity of inability, indeterminacy, indecision. Overcompensating, Eliot fills his poem with a clutter of "objective correlatives" for the state of feeling first dramatized by *Hamlet*. Eliot's spelling also significantly recalls his citation of Nerval's "la tour abolie" from "The Disinherited," in which the tower also figures in an Orphic tale that condenses the lover's and the artist's inconsolable fates in a shuttling between two worlds. Orpheus and Eurydice, by way of Hades and Persephone, cast a dark shadow across the mythic revivification of unity presided over by the poet-priest.

According to Eliot, the disinheritance of the modern poets occurred when feeling and intellect split, as they do in the "ordinary" mind. "When a poet's mind is perfectly equipped for its work, it is constantly amalgamating disparate experience; the ordinary man's experience is chaotic, irregular, fragmentary. The latter falls in love, or reads Spinoza, and these two experiences have nothing to do with each other, or with the noise of the typewriter or the smell of cooking: in the mind of the poet these experiences are always forming new wholes." J. Hillis Miller observes that these "*are* a miscellaneous lot," betraying Eliot's "feeling that experience is in fact chaotic" and harmonized only by "ironic conjunction." This miscellany, however, is no random choice, for it represents just those experiences that *The Waste Land* tries to set in order. In his essays on Leibniz (1916), Eliot's passing references to Spinoza are in the context of debates over the connections between mind and matter or body and soul. "Spinoza represents a definite emotional attitude," he asserts, leaving this attitude undefined, though we may infer a reference again to "Spinoza's naturalism . . . his disbelief in free will and immortality" and the "materialistic epiphenomenalism" of his "view of the relation of mind and body." Reading Spinoza plunges one into a deterministic "naturalism" that leaves little room for the soul to govern its responses to sensory influences. The doctrines of this heretical, exiled philosopher question the modality of a soul that would transcend, yet still involve, sensation—a doubt Eliot attempts to resolve by recourse to Aristotle and Bradley. Falling in love and the smell of cooking awaken the natural emotions and senses that lead to these dilemmas. From the "Preludes" to "Burbank with a Baedeker" and "Gerontion," Eliot explores the disturbing effects of sensory life on the orders of consciousness. Of course, it is up to the "noise of the typewriter" to write these feelings into a satisfying accord.

In *The Waste Land*, "whole of feeling" turns out to be an oxymoron since the emotions stirred in the various scenes of sterility, adultery, rape, lust, and purgation are decidedly unwholesome and destructive of harmony or coherence. When we examine the published poem alongside the manuscript drafts, such as the dirges and the portraits of ladies like Fresca and the duchess, we see more clearly than ever that the poem's many voices speak obsessively of the feelings inspired by sex and death, those two main enemies of the fortress of identity. As in Eliot's previous poetry, speakers and readers are made to suffer a morbid acuteness of the senses in scene after scene— the lilacs "breeding . . . out of the dead land"; "the brown fog of a winter dawn"; "her strange synthetic perfumes, / Unguent, powdered, or liquid—troubled, confused / And drowned the sense in odours"; "It's them pills I took, to bring it off "; "Silk handkerchiefs, cardboard boxes, cigarette ends / Or other testimony of summer nights"; "White bodies naked on the low damp ground"; "And bats with baby faces in the violet light." Eliot's fragments cohere chiefly in their physicality, in the music of their borrowed sounds and in the kinds of sensual experiences they represent. *The Waste Land*'s "symbols are not mystical, but emotional," wrote I. A. Richards, who called the poem "radically naturalistic." It composes a body, we might say, of sensory and poetic life, if indeed the two can be distinguished. The fragmentation of parts reenacts the *sparagmos* of the physical body of desire, torn by its conflicting responses to the excitements it tries to lift into the wholeness of meaning. Corresponding to these fractures is the poetic *sparagmos* of the body of the literary fathers—"And other withered stumps of time... told upon the walls"—toward whose sounds and feelings the poet reacts with a neurosis of the poetic libido, so to speak. Philomel's rape and dismemberment are supplemented by their change into "inviolable voice," but that sublation is now " 'Jug Jug' to dirty ears." Were we to clean up our response, what would we hear but the painful truth that her voice sings of the violence at its origin? Philomel's change and the metamorphosis of the father in Ariel's song figure the work of art as a transformation of loss into something rich and strange. While it seems to lament our incapacity to realize again such sublimations of the material into the spiritual, Eliot's poem also demonstrates that no "voice" is "inviolable." Even the play of syllables between those two words articulates the work of difference and interpenetration in language, and the location of identity in the rupture between things.

The "dissociation of sensibility" cataloged by Eliot's imagery traces the dissociation of individual senses from each other in the absence of any intellectual *Aufhebung* into a logos. There is a great irony, for example, in Eliot's assertion that "what Tiresias *sees*, in fact, is the substance of the poem." Tiresias' blindness should, according to myth, grant him a vision of the truth. What he "sees" in Eliot's poem is a troping of the primal scene in the mechanical copulation of the typist and the young man carbuncular. The metric, the rhyme scheme, and the ending sight of the "automatic hand" that "puts a record on the gramophone" enforce a feeling of remorseless repetition of a scene "foresuffered" a thousand times in memory and desire. Tiresias endlessly sees the scene of the crime, the origin of his own "blinding" or castration in witnessing the difference between men and women. What Tiresias sees is "substance" itself, physical life (or signifiers) unredeemed by spirit (or a transcendental signified). Eliot's note plays on the philosophic sense of "substance" as essence and tacitly reminds us of its declension into mere matter. In some legends, Tiresias loses his eyes in retaliation for looking upon the naked body of the bathing Athena, goddess of wisdom. In the version from Ovid that Eliot quotes as "of great anthropological interest," we have the tale of the coupling snakes,

Tiresias' bisexuality, and his blinding by Hera / Juno for answering that women enjoy sex nine times more than men. Of course, he is also the prophet of the dead in Hades, guide to sailors like Odysseus and Aeneas, and the seer who knows the fatal story of Oedipus. According to Eliot, he is "the most important personage in the poem, uniting all the rest." This unity will not cohere, however; Tiresias figures the mobility of sexual identity and the negative relation of what we see to what we know. To know the body of truth repeats the crime. Tiresias stands for the dissociation of sensibility in "all the rest" and everyone's participation in his pagan version of negative theology. What we see through his eyes is the involvement of transgression in the genesis of the logos. (Eliot's gramma-phone replays the old song recently rewritten by Derrida's gramatology.) A dissociation of sensibility sets in as the new prophet's "inviolable voice" sings out its reading of the writing of the oracular dead.

If we switch from mythological to other allegorical registers or codes of reference, we note that erection and resurrection also figure the *Aufhebung*, or blindness-made-vision, that achieves the "relevé," the raising of the dead or the return of what was invested in a threatening abyss. A castration logic, whereby loss is made the agency or origin of the logos, is the "system" that arranges Eliot's "bits of information." The dissemination of any single lyric speaker amid these babbling tongues seems to denote the final demise of the Romantic subject, but in fact the ventriloquial appropriation of dismembered parts remembered from other authors composes the new poet as an intertextual force. In these acts of loving violence toward the body of tradition, the poet resurfaces not as the origin of the poem but as the poetic principle (principal), the deconstructed genius loci of a textual waste land. The *sparagmos* as theme and method both expresses his dissociation by the daemons inhabiting his poetic landscape and exorcises those daemons by a ritual incorporation of their torn parts. Resemblance, correspondence, and other modes of identification predominate in the "cohesion" of the fragments, and they follow the practice of Lacan's "imaginary," or "mirror stage," discourse. The Father's No, Name, and Law have not been acceded to, the Oedipus complex (as the structure or language of the unconscious) has not dissolved, and a regression to the strategy of narcissism, doubling, identification, competition, and aggression has taken place. *The Waste Land* exhausts, and then will relinquish, the conceptual responses to sexual, philosophical, and poetic indeterminacy already introduced in "Prufrock," "Narcissus," and "Gerontion."

Translating Lacan's terms into poetics, we find that the "specific prematurity of birth," the child's "primordial Discord" and "motor-unco-ordination" become the young poet's incoherence. The mirror stage next provides cohesion through speculation. Recognizing his own image in that of others, the subject enters a drama "which manufactures for the subject, caught up in the lure of spatial iden-tification, the succession of fantasies that extends from a fragmented body image to a form of its totality." Images of the fragmented body recur when the symbolic systems of totalization give way, opening up a return to aggressive rivalry with the other for what both, because of their similarity, desire, so that such images connote at once a violence toward the other and a disintegration of self-identity: "These are the images of castration, mutilation, dismemberment, disloca-tion, evisceration, devouring, bursting open the body, in short, the *imagos* that I have grouped together under the apparently structural term of *imagos of the fragmented body*." In contrast, "the formation of the *I* is symbolized in dreams by a fortress, or a stadium—its inner arena and enclosure, surrounded by marshes and rubbish-tips, di-viding it into two opposed fields of contest where the subject floun-ders in quest of the lofty, remote inner castle whose form . . . symbolizes the id in a quite startling way." The Quester's journey to the Chapel Perilous marks the transition from the *sparagmos* of the God/king to the ritual decipherment of original mysteries, worked out by Eliot in his commentaries on the "DA" of the thunder.

The vocations of the Quester, detective, and critic merge in the attempt to solve once more the riddle of the sphinx or to recapture the sibyl's power to gather the scattering leaves into a logos—a power denied to Dante as he sought to express the vision of the Eternal Light and compared himself to the sibyl. The poem hesitates, like Hamlet, in the face of re-membering, torn between the idea of logos as the recollection of a lost absolute and logos as the emergence, in unauthorized directions, of beings gathered in their difference. The Heideggerian sense comes closer, I think, to Dante's single volume bound by love than Eliot's search for the Word of the Father, as a comparison to the end of "Little Gidding" will suggest. Love, as the call of being, remains open to the life that logocentrism forecloses. What we see with Tiresias throughout the poem is dead people, like scattered leaves, whirled beyond the bounds of love.

For the reader, the question becomes that of whether any in-terpretative ritual can, or should reunite the leaves of this *sparagmos* in a transcendental image of harmony. The trace of guilt that marks

Oedipus and the Quester suggests that acts of interpretation or divination are also acts of violence, that transgression may not be fully integrated when the truth is finally told. Unless we repeat it word for word, our critical account of the poem must always leave out something, must choose and select to form our solution to its riddle. Reading *The Waste Land* requires an interpretation that will also figure the tension between the desire to totalize and the need to criticize. One figure for the poem, then, is that of a corpus. The various definitions of *corpus* include 1) a physical body, especially when dead; 2) a structure constituting the main part of an organ; 3) the principal, or capital, as distinguished from the interest, or income, of a fund, estate, investment, or the like; 4) a large collection of writings of a specific kind or on a specific subject. As a critical metaphor, corpus makes the connection between a body of writing and a writing of or about the body. The representations of literature and sexuality in *The Waste Land* join in overdetermined settings, as Eliot draws upon the capital of a certain body of texts for his poetic treatment of failed passions, violent conquests, mechanical copulations, and purgative fires. In the strange logic of condensation, literary potency and sexual potency become a single problem, their result a common issue. The literary surrender of self that negatively produces an authorizing tradition coincides with images of emasculation that negatively body forth a sensation of the sexual sublime. In the metaphor of the corpus we may avoid imposing an a priori discrimination between sexuality and textuality, resist totalizing the poem's vital differences of detail in some metacritical order, and point toward the relations of crisis—between the body and writing, nature and culture, women and men, sons and fathers, talents and traditions—that sound throughout *The Waste Land*.

The critical detective discovers, then, that the corpus itself is a sphinx, an enigmatic collection of texts whose particular puzzle is the bond that joins the animal and the human and by extension the human and the divine. When we look into the corpus of *The Waste Land*, we do not find the identity of its owner, but instead the bric-a-brac from other writers' estates, or from the poet's past texts and memories. And the question those purloined letters pose is most often a variant of the sphinx's: what is man, if he should have such animal desires? What is the logos, that it can raise man's nature to its truth? What is a poet, that he presumes to place himself at such crossroads? The lines that open "The Burial of the Dead" place us before such oracular mysteries.

April is the cruellest month, breeding
Lilacs out of the dead land, mixing
Memory and desire, stirring
Dull roots with spring rain.

We can sketch with little difficulty the "self-reflexive" allegory of poetic beginnings in this overture. Though Eliot first intended a now-excised Boston night-town scene for his opener, the poem as published fortuitously contrasts with the beginning of Chaucer's *Canterbury Tales*, thus making English poetry new by turning the original celebration of fertility into an ode to dejection. "After great pain, a formal feeling comes," wrote Emily Dickinson, and in Eliot's lines a similar necessity of hurt seems involved in committing his feelings to form. "Winter kept us warm, covering / Earth in forgetful snow," a secure oblivion that seduces and comforts those who do not presume to begin writing again, who do not dare force the moment to its crisis. The meager quantity and the sorrowful content of so much of Eliot's poetry testify, as do his critical statements on daemonic possession, that writing was for him an anguish second only to the "acute discomfort" of feeling like a haunted house. Certainly one of the strongest of the obscure impulses behind *The Waste Land* is Eliot's recurring dread that his poetic springs have run dry. April stands for a new season of poetic creation, "breeding" poems out of the detritus of his literary inheritance and notebook drafts. His memory of past glories (his own and others, for as signs of poetic achievement they come to the same thing) obsesses him, cruelly blocking his desire to engender some new flowering. As a rendition of the Anglican burial service, Eliot's opening inters the corpus of the fathers, buries them to sprout according to his own pronouncements. While it tropes against the poets and metaphors of natural regeneration, it also laments (and so in a sense denies) its own impotence. "Dull roots" characterizes the literary ancestry and the poet's own instrument of creation.

In these lines and throughout the poem, we encounter the same overdetermination of Eliot's rhetoric seen in his critical accounts of poetic genesis. The foregoing poetic allegory already employs terms that lead into an interpretation of the passage as an allegory of sexuality. April denotes the awakening of passion, the surge of desire to break out of the cold forgetfulness of repression. Memories cruelly block the fulfillment of desire, as the dead hand of past experiences—formed by the history of the unconscious—reaches out to obstruct present feelings. Prufrock had invoked the figure of Lazarus, come back from the dead to tell us all, to signify an intercourse he never dares begin. In *The Waste Land*, resurre(re)ction is no "friend to men," since it draws them out of the winter warmth of indifference and into the world of nature, woman, and history. Corresponding with the refinement of the poet's nature by his surrender to the voices of the dead, desire seeks a fiery sublimation that also takes its cue from the figure of Arnaut Daniel, one of Dante's tongues of flame who undergoes a transfiguration into Buddha and Saint Augustine at the end of "The Fire Sermon."

The analysis could be further extended, with appropriate precautions, by invoking the Dantean model, explicated in the letter to Can Grande, of the "polysemous" text so influential in Eliot's method. At the literal level is the poetic exodus from anxiety; at the moral level is the salvation from the death of the soul in lust; at the allegorical level is the soul's ascension from earth to heaven; at the anagogical level is the union of logos and nature in the Corpus Mysticum, or celestial church body, that regathers the saved in the volume of the Word. If there has been a murder here, if author, reader, and Quester join in a single detective adventure, it concerns the discovery of a Corpus Mysticum resolving these various levels in a single thunderous apocalypse that crosses the aporia between nature and the logos.

Eliot's attraction to Catholicism as it emerges in the poem may well turn on the transcendental poetics its theology offers. In contrast to the iconoclasm of Hebrew, Protestant, and Puritan theories of the sign, Catholicism reunites the letter and the spirit, signifier and signified, nature and culture, human and divine in the dogmas of the Incarnation, Passion, and Resurrection. The fertility rituals would be a type to the antitype of the Sacrament, as indeed the Grail legends imply. Following traditional theological exegesis, the waters of *The Waste Land* are both the baptismal river and the blood of the Eucharist. Echoing Dante, these waters mark the entrance to a regenerated Earthly Paradise at the end of purgatory. The first three sections of the poem constitute a kind of preparation of the soul and heart for reception of the Word, adopting from mystic literature their climactic call for a prerequisite purification or celibacy before the final approach to the mystery. The final two sections, written at the last and chiefly at Lausanne, move away from the vegetation ritual schema into two related models—those of the quest and the elegy—

to resolve the puzzle. What is achieved thereby is a powerful revision of the precursors as Eliot thinks poetically through the structures of negative theology, but he never finds his Beatrice. The poem leaves us at the edge of purgatory but still far distant from paradise, lacking that loving logos that moved the constellations of Dante and that returns in the brightest moments of the *Quartets*.

Eliot, Russell, and Whitman: Realism, Politics, and Literary Persona in *The Waste Land*

Cleo McNelly Kearns

Wyndham Lewis, one of the most penetrating critics of T. S. Eliot's early literary career (and one to whom Eliot's recent biographers should pay more attention), remarked of Eliot that he was "democratic in spite of himself." Eliot, he went on to argue, had "imbibed more than his share of romantically 'radical' values in his tender years," and his classical panache, as Lewis liked to call it, together with his deliberately Gallic pose—"a bit of *le dandy* as inherited from Baudelaire"—was rather a disguise than a genuine point of view. Radical or no radical, Eliot knew that the contemporary Anglo-Saxon world of arts and letters was "half Marx and half *status quo*," and his early position in aesthetics, if not in politics proper, was more deeply influenced by Bertrand Russell's progressive realism than others who did not know him might suspect. In general, for Lewis, Eliot's position within the world of letters smacked too much of scientism, not to mention a democratization of art fostered by Pound, to be of much comfort to the genuine conservative. Because both Eliot and Pound stressed the need for technique, and attempted to spell out what that technique involved, they reduced art to mechanics, and made it accessible, as Lewis so charmingly puts it, to "anyone certified born of woman, indeed to any son-of-a-bitch" (*Men Without Art*).

Eliot, of course, having more sense, did not go quite so far as Pound in this democratic "manufacture of poets." At least, Lewis

---

notes, Eliot managed to keep from puffing the reputations of *quite* so many losers, and showed nothing like Pound's ability to gather the dubiously "discipular" around him. Nevertheless, Lewis insisted that the separation of belief, personality, and class (and gender) identity from the work of art itself, on which Eliot insisted, cooperated, intentionally or not, with the apparently leftward slide of history. The effective divorce of *The Waste Land* from the belief, the ethos, the social and personal position of its author would make of it, Lewis remarked, his tone dripping acid, a "posthumous ornament," a "feather" in Eliot's cap, a dubious but effective "passport to the communist millennium."

Rightly or wrongly, the judgment of most recent critics about the political implications of Eliot's early career has been quite the reverse of Lewis's. Eliot's separation of issues of personality, personal identity and belief from issues of poetic mastery and strength, far from speeding a leftward slide in history or even a progressive point of view, has seemed to shore up a kind of literary and political conservatism. At the very least, it has prevented critics—or so the argument usually goes—from correcting for "Anglo-Saxony," with its class, race, sexual and even national bias, by paying special attention to work which emanates, biographically and socially, from other sources and points of view. This consensus, not to be lightly dismissed, nevertheless leaves us with an anomaly which critics have always recognized: how could so conservative a view, both in aesthetics and in politics in the larger sense, possibly have produced a text like *The Waste Land*? Whatever cries of elitism and reaction may have risen in the wake of this poem, its initial reception and its continuing impact—not least (as many critical reviews and poems testify) on third-world cultures and on an increasingly literate working class—prevent us from ever completely forgetting its great force as one of the most politically and culturally subversive texts of our century.

Given this anomaly, it may be worth reconsidering Lewis's point of view, or at least attempting to understand a little better the cultural and political matrix that allowed him to put it forth. After all, Lewis had the great advantage not only of knowing Eliot well but of knowing the kinds of conversation—about politics, about art, and no doubt about sex—on which his mind was trained. Whatever rhetorical posturing Lewis himself may have indulged in here, and however hostile he himself was to the portrait he so vividly drew, he was certainly giving us an image very different from the tailored, bowler-hatted Establishment figure we have come to accept as Eliot. To see Eliot's oft-depicted formality as the formality of a dandy rather than that of a Chairman of the Board is revealing, and to further sketch the American democrat under the Gallic poseur is to recast even that image in a new form. Lewis's remarks, polemical as they are, force us to consider at least the possibility that Eliot did indeed have deep and deeply disguised impulses toward radical politics, philosophical realism, and that sexual freedom with which they were often associated in his time, and that these impulses had aesthetic consequences, both in his theory and in his poetry. Ideas, impulses, and directions so different from his official position were, of course, troubling, and Eliot often recognized them indirectly, if at all. Nevertheless, if we look briefly at two important figures in his life, Bertrand Russell and Walt Whitman, and then glance again, equally briefly, at *The Waste Land*, we can trace in Eliot's artistic lineage not only the metaphysical and French symbolist traditions of which he so often spoke, but another, deeper line of descent, one in which the democratic, the sexually open and the philosophically realist views of his greatest mentors take on a new and potentially fruitful life.

Both in Russell's work and in Whitman's, Eliot found a highly mediated, self-reflexive, idealist, and abstract approach to previous texts or philosophical problems challenged and superceded by a new, direct and even sensual apprehension of what we might call, with appropriate caveats and reservations, the "real." In both writers, too, these direct, open, democratically accessible and sense-affirming views were linked with an explicit sexual politics, a politics of "free love," to use the now somewhat dated term, or at least of tremendous sexual affirmation, which Eliot found both disturbing and vital. They were also, and in Eliot's view, less fortunately, allied with an inflated and sometimes sentimental rhetorical style, which was often embarrassingly fatuous or disconcertingly self-revealing, or both. Hence the vogue Eliot himself created for a metaphysical, witty and Gallic poetry, distanced and ironic, even in its treatment of sexuality or of the Eastern traditions was, even as he created it, in part a mask or defense to cover his lifelong agonistic struggle with a very different, even antithetical, style and point of view.

To take the philosophical position first, Russell (and to some extent Santayana as well) represented, for Eliot, a realist position in philosophy, together with a political and sexual point of view which challenged both the Bradleyan idealism of his graduate training and his own conservative instincts. More important, the perspectives opened up by Russell's neorealist philosophy offered the possibility of a new poetics, a poetics of direct sensual apprehension of ideas. Indeed, as Russell frequently testified, his break with idealism and his beginning exploration of a realist point of view had an aesthetic dimension even for the philosophers themselves. When he and Moore suddenly understood, Russell says, that the "meaning of an idea" was "something wholly independent of mind," they both experienced a sense of "emancipation." Though each was later to qualify this view in important ways, the memory of its releasing power did not fade. Importantly for Eliot, Russell's sense of release was occasioned directly by a break with Bradley, who had been his teacher and on whose system he, like Eliot, had formed his first philosophical thought. Later in life, Russell wrote:

> Bradley argued that everything common sense believes in is mere appearance; we reverted to the opposite extreme, and thought that *everything* is real that common sense, uninfluenced by philosophy or theology, supposes real. With a sense of escaping from prison, we allowed ourselves to think that grass is green, that the sun and stars would exist if no one was aware of them, and also that there is a pluralistic timeless world of Platonic ideas. The world, which had been thin and logical, suddenly became rich and varied and solid. Mathematics could be *quite* true, and not merely a stage in a dialectic.

Eliot's most important early critical formulations, the notion of the mind of the poet as a "shred of platinum," the idea of the "objective correlative," even the famous "dissociation of sensibility," can be traced less to his idealist mentors (though there are influences from Royce and Bradley in all of them) than to the new influence of realism. Idealism may have set the terms of his thought, but that drive for a sensual image which would form a direct link to and a necessary invocation of a given train of thought and feeling, that desperate desire to escape from the extreme textuality, the infinite regress, of post-Hegelian idealism, that search for a language which would be "quite true," and not merely a pragmatic tool or a stage in an endless, verbal dialectic, are all motivated by new winds, not old ones. As Santayana so well understood, the new realism could motivate not only a negative rejection of New England Puritanism, or Germanic textuality, but a positive movement as well: a movement toward that "sense of beauty," that aesthetic view of the world, which would be, in its own way, as "rich, and varied and solid" as Russell's. When this movement was allied with the search for a language which would represent it in as precise and compelling a way as a logical symbol or mathematic equation, the combination was heady indeed.

Russell's presence in Eliot's life was itself "rich and varied and solid"—and complex. Russell came to lecture at Harvard in 1914 in Eliot's last year of residence as a graduate student, at a time when that august institution had just lost or was about to lose its giants: Royce and James. The importance of what Russell had to give, both in terms of academic politics and in terms of substance, was not lost on his colleagues, and his presence was courted on every side. Eliot was one of several advanced students presented for his delectation, and he was encouraged to take Russell's course in logic, finding it less than central to his development, but enjoying the sense of "pleasure and power" gained by "manipulating [those] curious little figures." Eliot and some other senior students took advantage of Russell's desire to meet with the brightest young Americans in a tutorial situation, and their ease and confidence before the visitor from abroad, while charming Russell himself, occasioned quite a little flurry among more timid souls. Russell's judgment of Eliot, that he was brilliant, but did not have the temperament of a philosopher, was not an imperceptive one, and their encounter proved the beginning of a vexed but important friendship.

Russell quickly became, much to his own and Eliot's delight, a problematic figure at Harvard. He represented points of view which were new and challenging not only in philosophical but in sexual and political terms as well, and whatever he represented, he did so at maximum force. His aristocratic background and his impeccable credentials made it hard for Cambridge, Massachusetts, to ignore his advanced position on the equality of women and on "free love," and he drew down upon himself a great deal of attention, compounded in equal parts of awe and nerves. If his poetry is any indication, Eliot reveled in Russell's iconoclastic descent into Massachusetts society, and he recorded the resulting comedy of manners in his poem "Mr. Apollinax." The poem was occasioned by a weekend at a house party given by Anglophile academics. Eliot, who attended, associated Russell ever after with with a certain faunlike sexuality, with a general stirring of the kinds of desires, fantasies, and images such occasions usually exclude. He enjoyed presenting, in his poem, this troubling sense of a more sexually charged, more alive, less well-repressed world, together with the faint sense of social contretemps which hung in the air. He was vividly struck with Russell's physical appearance (his tiny stature, his pointed ears, his undeniable sexual force) and did not fail to associate these accidents of nature with Russell's philosophical point of view. Both the liberated attitude toward sexuality Russell exemplified and his challenge to the predominant idealism of Harvard's philosophy department were part of what made his position "modern." It was a serious position, and Eliot recognized it as such, in spite of the comedy, and of later reference to Russell as a "priapic" materialist, or in punning terms as a "depressing life-forcer."

"Mr. Apollinax" exemplifies a good deal of that mixture of "stylistic effrontery" and secret fascination with a peculiarly radical and open point of view in Eliot detected by Wyndham Lewis. The poem makes use of Russell's power to stir a number of evocative images, and yet masks the interest of its young writer in these with an overtone of irony, a certain Gallic distance. In presenting images of Russell as an "irresponsible foetus," with laughter "submarine and profound," associated with the "beat of centaur's hoofs," while at the same time mentioning, in wry dismissal, that Professor and Mrs. Channing-Cheetah stimulated only memories of a "slice of lemon, and a bitten macaroon," Eliot was commenting on the power, for poetry, of a certain philosophical, sexual, and political position as well as on the necessity (for him) to frame that position with a certain irony. Russell's later friendship with Eliot and his first wife in London confirmed both these associations and the reservations Eliot was quite right to maintain, and even after they drew apart, Eliot continued to treat both Russell and his point of view with the respect they deserved.

Any disturbing impulses provoked by the party at the Channing-Cheetahs and its aftermath were as nothing, for Eliot, compared with the challenges posed by his reading of the work of Whitman. Russell, after all, was a philosopher, and he offered Eliot no competition whatsoever when it came to his real vocation, the writing of poetry. Whitman, by contrast, was a poet, a great one, and one of Eliot's own line of descent. Antithetical in temperament, taste and technique to Eliot, Whitman shared with him not only a profound engagement with Eastern thought, especially that of the *Bhagavad Gita*, but a transcendental heritage, an interest in realism, and, at least at first, a prophetic sense of vocation as well. For both, too, this early prophetic sense quickly modulated into elegy, as each confronted the collapse of that hope for a new culture through the depredations of modern war. In spite—or perhaps because of—his loose, open, self-revealing style and the risks of content and form he took, Whitman focused for Eliot the tensions he felt between the stance of the American democrat as wisdom poet and universal sage and that of the Gallic aristocrat as metaphysician, dandy and invulnerable wit.

Eliot testified to his ambivalence toward Whitman in terms so reminiscent of Harold Bloom's *Anxiety of Influence* as to be somewhat uncanny, and Bloom's work is perhaps the best theoretical guide both to Eliot's relationship to this precursor and to the way in which it informs *The Waste Land* itself. In a review essay of 1926, for instance, Eliot constructed a classic defense against Whitman's fathering power by comparing him unfavorably to Baudelaire, that *semblable* and *frère*, whose precedent was neither so immediate (taking place as it did in another language) nor so threatening (representing, as it did, at least for Eliot, a classic, heterosexual, and even orthodox point of view). Baudelaire, Eliot argued, understood the great gap, the abyss, between the real and the ideal which yawns especially wide whenever the identity or even the direct connection between the deep self and the outside world is asserted. Whitman did not understand this gap; indeed, he blurred and sentimentalized the line between self and other, perception and truth. Even his much-vaunted sexual frankness, Eliot argued (quite unjustifiably), did not come from courage or honesty but simply from the relatively uncritical insouciance of an assertive nature in a permissive milieu. Whitman had refused, as it were, to "look into the abyss" opened by his own ideas; there was, for him, no "chasm" between the real and the ideal such as opened before the "horrified" eyes of Baudelaire. As a result, Whitman had neither discipline nor the right to speak of it, and he compromised both his material and his own poetic strength ("Whitman and Tennyson"). Eliot rejected the weak stance he associated with Whitman here less for reasons of prudence or prudery than because he simply could not bear to contemplate the kind of vulnerability, both in theory and in practice, Whitman's "blurring of the line" entailed. The possibility that surrender might be reduced to seduction, openness to the world to slavery to sense impressions, and poetic affirmation to the self-inflated rhetoric of what Bloom calls the American Baroque Defeat, was one his own life and thought had brought him to recognize at every turn. To reveal any connection whatever between self and persona was to court the annihilation of both, either by the professorate on the one hand or by the object of one's bewildered desires on the other. The history of this fear and its strong locus in the figure of Whitman was encoded, for Eliot, in the suppressed and very early poem "Ode" from *Ara Vos Prec*. The poem records in cryptic form a moment of intense sexual de-idealization and poetic collapse, haunted on the one side by the submarine laughter of the realist/satyr/Russell figure we have already seen in "Mr. Apollinax" and on the other by the bubbling of an uninspired Mephitic [female?] river. Between them lies a deadly, misread Whitmanian text, identified by Whitman's own synedoche of the calamus or pond reed.

In general, in his early reaction to Whitman, Eliot shows, as he does in this desperate little verse, more than a touch of phobia—perhaps even homophobia. By declaring, prematurely, the father's impotence, he reveals his own poetic and psychological weakness all the more clearly. It would be wrong, however, to reduce his reactions entirely to the level of repression or even the more self-interested kinds of defensiveness. As he elsewhere testified, Eliot believed that Whitman had identified the ideal and the real too closely and conjoined them too closely, as well, with motives of rhetorical and sexual display. In doing so, Eliot felt, he had put his poetry at risk. To the distrust produced by this risk, Eliot could add his own political suspicion of Whitman's courting of the many, the crowd, what Whitman himself liked to call the "En-mass." When Eliot took refuge beneath the masks of Laforgue, Corbière, and Baudelaire, then, he was defending himself both against the phantoms of fathering omnipotence in Whitman and against legitimate dangers and fears, including fears of that mass culture which sought to reduce them both to caricatures of themselves.

Even as he formulated this defensive stance, however, Eliot was capable of hearing in Whitman another, stronger voice. Again, we can see this more clearly by looking at his changing views of other poets, particularly of Baudelaire. By 1930, Eliot was beginning to see or admit to problems in Baudelaire. Baudelaire had achieved the awareness that no object is equal to human desire, Eliot argued in his essay of that year, but he had not attained to the belief that there exists, beyond the material world, a further object equal to that desire. He had not, that is, as Eliot put it, "learned to look to *death* for what life cannot give." Whitman had done precisely this, in his great odes to death. Of Whitman, Eliot elsewhere wrote at about this time: "beneath all the declamations there is another tone, and behind all the illusions there is another vision." For Eliot, that tone and vision surfaced in Whitman's (very American) images of mocking bird and lilac, and he heard them, too, if *The Waste Land* is testimony, in the voice of the hermit thrush, caroling "death's outlet song of life."

Eliot was able fully to admit the greatness of Whitman, however, only after he had to come to terms with his own American identity and achieved that poetic mastery on his own terms which gave him the security to confront his precursor again. The problem was clearly one of influence in the Bloomian sense, and Eliot often put it in just these terms. During the course of an essay called "American Literature and American Language" written in 1953, (in *To Criticize the Critic*) Eliot took up the question of influence explicitly, and he did so, significantly, in the context of a consideration of Whitman, Twain, and Poe. For models to *imitate*, Eliot said, a writer will often go to (usually minor) writers of another country and another language. By contrast, the great writers of the immediate past in his own tradition will function largely as "something definite to rebel against." There is a distinction, however, Eliot went on to argue, between genuine "influence" and the imitation of models or styles. "A true disciple is impressed by what his master has to say," he wrote, "and *consequently* by his way of saying it; an imitator—I might say a borrower—is impressed chiefly by the way his master said it." In this sense, Eliot was an "imitator" or "borrower" from the French, but he was a *disciple* of the Americans, and particularly of Whitman. Furthermore, by his own testimony, his discipleship had to do primarily with "what Whitman had to say" and only consequently with "how he said it."

"What Whitman had to say" involved, as we have seen, both radical democracy and sexual politics, and it also involved, crucially for Eliot, a certain very distinct, cogent and challenging reading of Eastern thought. While he seems to have been innocent of very much direct contact with Eastern texts, and innocent as well of the kinds of epistemological despair that they raised in both earlier and later orientalists, Whitman had nevertheless achieved, by his maturity, a remarkable, original and culturally prescient understanding of one tendency in the Eastern traditions. That understanding, as recent critics of the relation between American and Hindu thought have increasingly stressed (V. K. Chari, Beongcheon Yu), was highly realist in terms of its Western orientation, rather than representing in a familiar way the philosophical idealism to which Eastern texts are more frequently assimilated in the West. Whitman's importance for Eliot, then, certainly lay in his understanding, inherent in the *Bhagavad Gita*, among other texts, but often overlooked there, of a detached but affirmative relation to sense experience, of an exoteric and culturally open approach to philosophical and religious truth, and of the validity of the active as well as the contemplative life. Eliot was never more Whitman's "disciple" than in his ability to envision in Eastern texts something more compelling, more disturbing and ultimately more liberating than mere denunciations of the world of appearance as pure illusion.

Whitman's realist and affirmative views and Russell's break with idealism had, then, not only great philosophical but great aesthetic and political weight for Eliot. The direction of their thought, however, and the styles in which it was embodied, were antithetical to his temperament and cast of mind. In order to work through these problems, Eliot had first to create a space for himself by the development of an original and opposing style and then to allow the "influence" of his mentors to flow into his own work in a strong, but thoroughly mastered and assimilated way.

One result of this poetic project was *The Waste Land*, a difficult and disturbing poem which has been read, no doubt with some justification, both as the already-dated and highly subjective product of the personal traumas of a bourgeois litterateur and as the most advanced and indeed subversive of modernist texts. To I. A. Richards fell the lot of being first to articulate the latter position, and his terribly modern *Waste Land*, was, no doubt, part of the provocation which made Eliot, in reaction, call it no more than a piece of "rhythmic grumbling." Even as a piece of "rhythmic grumbling," however, *The Waste Land*'s force has not always been lost, even on the discourse of the left. If the poem has not become, as Lewis sardonically predicted, a "passport to the communist millennium," it has at least fulfilled something of Trotsky's 1924 mandate for art. It has, that is, found "the necessary rhythm of words for dark and vague moods"; it has brought "thought and feeling closer"; it has enriched "the spiritual experience of the individual and of the community"; and this it has done "quite independently of whether it appears in a given case under the flag of a 'pure' or of a frankly tendentious art" ("The Formalist School"). We could do worse than to follow Trotsky's lead here, and look to the poem not at all to "incriminate" its author with the thoughts and feelings which he expresses but rather to "ask" to which order of feelings his work corresponds, what are its social and historical coordinates, and above all "what literary heritage has entered into the elaboration of the new form?"

A partial answer to the latter question is certainly found in the remarkable series of allusions to the work of Whitman which inform *The Waste Land*, and are especially marked in its final movement. Together, the heritage of Whitman and that of the Upanishads provide a channel through which a radical, open, democratic, and accessible voice rises in counterpoint and resolution to the closed, metaphysical, and guarded style which appears to dominate Eliot's early work. It is true that these allusions, especially in the case of Whitman, are largely unacknowledged. Eliot's note on the "hermit thrush," whose song is heard in Part V, and whose voice, as we shall see, is so clearly an echo of the same bird who sings in "When Lilacs Last in the Dooryard Bloom'd," directs us not to a previous text, in Whitman or elsewhere, but to the "real" bird of the American Northeast. This suppression of Whitman's name, however, whether unconscious or deliberate, is part of a movement toward direct representation and affirmative feeling which seeks to escape from the infinite regress of textual allusions which seems to pervade the poem and to find the "objective correlative," the conjunction of sound and sense, signified and signifier, knowledge and experience, of which Whitman spoke in different terms, and which he, too, sought to embody.

John Hollander and Harold Bloom have repeatedly drawn attention to the extended and systematic echoes of Whitman in *The Waste Land* (Gauss Lectures, 1981; *Figure of Echo*). The full impact of these can only be measured, however, by laying "When Lilacs Last in the Dooryard Bloom'd" side by side with Eliot's text. Here, then, are a few of the relevant passages from Whitman, beginning

with portions of the opening, moving through the song of the hermit
thrush to the lyrical celebration of the American city (of which Eliot's
London is a travesty) and ending with the final journey, the poet's
last walk along the "long black trail," where he becomes the third
of three companions, the other two the "thought of death and the
knowledge of death," wending their way to the place of revelation
among the "dark cedars and ghostly pines."

> When lilacs last in the dooryard bloom'd,
> And the great star early droop'd in the western sky in
>   the night,
> I mourn'd, and yet shall mourn with ever-returning
>   spring.
> . . . .
> In the swamp in secluded recesses,
> A shy and hidden bird is warbling a song.
>
> Solitary the thrush,
> The hermit withdrawn to himself, avoiding the
>   settlements,
> Sings by himself a song.
>
> Song of the bleeding throat,
> Death's outlet song of life, (for well dear brother I
>   know,
> If thou wast not granted to sing thou would'st surely
>   die.)
> . . . .
> Coffin that passes through lanes and streets,
> Through day and night with the great cloud
>   darkening the land,
> With the pomp of the inloop'd flags with the cities
>   draped in black,
> With the show of the States themselves as of crape-
>   veil'd women
>   standing,
> With processions long and winding and the flambeaus
>   of the night,
> With the countless torches lit, with the silent sea of
>   faces and the

unbared heads.

. . . .

—where amid these you journey,
With the tolling tolling bells' perpetual clang,
Here, coffin that slowly passes,
I give you my sprig of lilac.

. . . .

Falling upon them all and among them all, enveloping
          me with the
          rest
Appear'd the cloud, appear'd the long black trail,
And I knew death, its thought, and the sacred
          knowledge of death.
Then with the knowledge of death as walking one
          side of me,
And the thought of death close-walking the other side
          of me,
And I in the middle as with companions, and as
          holding the hands of companions,
I fled forth to the hiding receiving night that talks not,
Down to the shores of the water, the path by the
          swamp in the dimness.
To the solemn shadowy cedars and ghostly pines so
          still.

And the singer so shy to the rest receiv'd me,
The gray-brown bird I know receiv'd us comrades
          three,
And he sang the carol of death, and a verse for him I
          love.

. . . .

And the voice of my spirit tallied the song of the bird.

. . . .

I saw battle-corpses, myriads of them,
And the white skeletons of young men, I saw them,
I saw the debris and debris of all the slain soldiers of
          the war,
But I saw they were not as was thought,
They themselves were fully at rest, they suffer'd not,
The living remain'd and suffer'd, the mother suffer'd,

> And the wife and the child and the musing comrade
>   suffer'd,
> And the armies that remained suffer'd.

Whitman's poem gives us not only the motifs and images of
The Waste Land, from the lilacs and flowers through the "unreal city"
to the disturbing thought of the bodies of dead soldiers, the presence
of a double self, a dear brother or *semblable*, the "murmur of maternal
lamentation," the peering faces, and the song of the hermit thrush
over the dry bones, but its very tone and pace, the steady andante
which makes of both poems a walking meditation. We are not far
here from Eliot's themes and tone in Part V:

> After the torchlight red on sweaty faces
> After the frosty silence in the gardens
> After the agony in stony places
> The shouting and the crying
> Prison and palace and reverberation
> Of thunder of spring over distant mountains
> He who was living is now dead
> We who were living are now dying
> With a little patience

Even Whitman's "thought of death" and "knowledge of death,"
who with him form three companions, seems to herald Eliot's "third
who walks always beside you," that ambiguous figure which seems
also, like the "singer shy to the rest," half-projection, half-reality,
emerging and disappearing into that intermediate zone "where the
hermit thrush sings in the pine trees."

What allows Whitman's poetry to flow into Eliot's here is a
conjunction not simply of voice but of conscious theme and subconscious psychic preoccupation as well. Both poems move at the
boundary between East and West, both approach, with a sense of
danger and sacrifice, the great assertion of the identity of the deep
self with the divine, fully realized only in and through both a literal
and a metaphorical death. For both, that assertion must, if it is to
be effective, take place in a material form and have real, physical,
and emotional implications. Both are mourning the death of a father
figure, with all such mourning implies of violence, ambivalence,
self-sacrifice, and pain, and both are seeking a simplicity, a sobriety
of expression which will reflect both Wordsworth's "awful power

to chasten and subdue" and the equal power to elevate and establish their own poetic identities. Both, furthermore, find that simplicity in sound, in incantation, in chant or "carol" as Whitman calls it, in the intonations of a voice which comes as much from without as from within the egocentric, personal, daily self. At the end, too, both break into great incantations which unclose the eyes and provide a new vision of the dead, no longer threatening to break decaying from the ground, but become, as *The Waste Land* puts it, "dry bones" which "harm no one" because the closed and self-conscious personal self that animated them is at rest.

Eliot's poem, moreover, juxtaposes the "dear brother" of Whitman's "When Lilacs Last in the Dooryard Bloom'd," with the "*semblable*" and "*frère*" of Baudelaire's *L'Ennui*. He thus brings into sharp tension his Gallic, metaphysical and antithetical mask and his open, vulnerable plea for a democratic fraternity of poets. Whitman's "dear brother" is, of course, as the poem goes on to make clear, the hermit thrush, whose "song of the bleeding throat" is "death's outlet song of life." The voice of that bird is heard in Eliot's "water-dripping" song, and *The Waste Land* measures the cost of the suppression and subsequent release of this song, which springs from a "bleeding throat," at other points as well. For Eliot, too, song arises from a violation; the "bleeding throat" is matched by the rape of Philomela, metamorphosed into the nightingale, whose voice is "inviolable." Philomela, like Whitman, has learned to "look to death for what life cannot give," and only in contemplating her example—and in "musing on the king my brother's wreck"—can the poem harmonize its "real and its ideal needs."

When, however, in its closing lines, *The Waste Land* breaks into the line *quando fiam uti chelidon*, it seems, even at this late and desperate moment, to guard, at least under the disguise of Latin, that pose of classical panache of which Wyndham Lewis had scornfully spoken. This is not the cry of the "democrat in spite of himself" but of the far more careful and controlled *defensor fidei*, the one who has paid, as Lewis put it, "a great deal of curious attention to the sanctions required for the expression of the thinking subject in verse or prose." The content, however, belies the form. "When will I be as the swallow," the verse cries out, linking its cry not only to the song of Philomela, but to Whitman's thrush as well. Whitman's poem looms again here, providing at once a gloss and antiphon to Eliot's, one in which his particular form of defensive self-protection has been utterly forgone. It is toward Eliot, as well as toward the hermit thrush, that Whitman proleptically moves when he calls out in answer to that cry: "For well dear brother I know, / If thou wast not granted to sing thou would'st surely die."

In his relation to Whitman, seen in the context of the thought of Russell, and indeed of the Upanishadic tradition as well, Eliot seeks, before our half-horrified, half-enamoured eyes, to cross the gap or abyss that separates the radical democrat from the Gallic poseur, the sexually free from the sexually contorted or repressed, the poetically accessible and fraternal from the poetically Oedipal and closed, the esoteric and philosophically idealist from the exoteric and realist position. That chasm cannot be easily traversed, and only in recognition of its depth can we make any sense at all of the contradictions in Eliot's work. Eliot's early career, more than that of any other modernist, dramatizes the difficult problem of translation involved when we seek to turn a mental and philosophical image of liberation into the objective reality of political, sexual, and aesthetic release. To have reminded us that such a translation involves prior acts of control, restraint, and sacrifice, and that it must stand up under the acerbic gaze of a Wyndham Lewis as well as under the apparently more benign scrutiny of a Leavis or a Richards, is not the least of Eliot's achievements.

Chronology

1670	Andrew Eliot, T. S. Eliot's ancestor, emigrated from East Coker, Somerset, to settle in Massachusetts.
1834	Rev. William Greenleaf Eliot (Unitarian), T. S. Eliot's grandfather, settled in St. Louis, Missouri.
1888	Thomas Stearns Eliot born September 26, in St. Louis. Youngest of seven children born to Henry Ware Eliot and Charlotte Eliot (née Stearns).
1906–10	Undergraduate at Harvard. Discovered the Symbolists and Laforgue. An editor of the *Harvard Advocate*, a literary magazine.
1910–12	Studied in Paris at the Sorbonne. Visited Germany. Wrote "Preludes," "Prufrock," "Portrait of a Lady," "Rhapsody on a Windy Night," and "La Figlia che Piange."
1911–14	Graduate student in philosophy at Harvard. Began dissertation on the philosophy of F. H. Bradley.
1914	Study at the University of Marburg, Germany, cut off by war. Residence at Merton College, Oxford. Met Ezra Pound.
1915–16	"Prufrock" published in *Poetry*, in Chicago, and in *Blast*, in England, 1915. Teaching and reviewing in London. Completed Bradley thesis. Married to Vivien Haigh-Wood, 1915.
1917–19	Employee of Lloyd's Bank. Assistant Editor of *The Egoist*. *Prufrock and Other Observations*, 1917. "Tradition and the Individual Talent," 1919.
1920	*Poems* and *The Sacred Wood*. Began *The Waste Land*.
1922	Became editor of *The Criterion*, a position he held until it folded in 1939. Dial Award for *The Waste Land*.

153

1924	"Four Elizabethan Dramatists."
1925	"The Hollow Men" and *Poems, 1909-25*. Joined Faber & Gwyer, later Faber & Faber, publishers.
1926	Two "Fragments" (of *Sweeney Agonistes*).
1927–31	Became a member of the Church of England and a British citizen, 1927. *Ariel Poems*, 1927–31. *For Lancelot Andrewes*, 1928. "Ash-Wednesday," 1930. *Coriolan*, 1931. *Thoughts after Lambeth*, 1931.
1932–33	First visit to America since 1914. Delivered Charles Eliot Norton Lectures at Harvard (published as *The Use of Poetry and the Use of Criticism*, 1933), and the Page-Barbour Lectures at the University of Virginia (published as *After Strange Gods—A Primer of Modern Heresy*, 1934). *Selected Essays*. Break-up of first marriage.
1934	*The Rock*.
1935–36	*Murder in the Cathedral*. *Collected Poems, 1909–35*, including "Burnt Norton," 1936.
1939	Delivered the Cambridge Lectures, published as *The Idea of a Christian Society*. *The Family Reunion*.
1940–44	*Four Quartets*, 1943. Part time fire-watcher, 1940–41. "What Is a Classic?," 1944.
1946	Lectured in Washington. Visited Ezra Pound at St. Elizabeths Hospital. Moved into apartment in London he was to share with John Hayward until 1957.
1947	Honorary degree from Harvard. Death of first wife, after long illness.
1948	Awarded the Order of Merit and the Nobel Prize for Literature. *Notes Towards a Definition of Culture*.
1950	*The Cocktail Party*.
1951	Suffered a mild heart attack. In poor health thereafter.
1954–55	Awarded the Hanseatic Goethe Prize, 1954. *The Confidential Clerk*.
1956	Lectured in Minneapolis on "The Frontiers of Criticism."
1957	*On Poetry and Poets*. Married Valerie Fletcher, his personal secretary.
1959	*The Elder Statesman*.
1961	Lectured at Leeds, published as "To Criticize the Critic."
1962–63	Seriously ill in London. Visited New York with Valerie Eliot, 1963.
1965	Died in London, January 4.

Contributors

HAROLD BLOOM, Sterling Professor of the Humanities at Yale University, is the author of *The Anxiety of Influence, Poetry and Repression*, and many other volumes of literary criticism. His forthcoming study, *Freud: Transference and Authority*, attempts a full-scale reading of all of Freud's major writings. A MacArthur Prize Fellow, he is general editor of five series of literary criticism published by Chelsea House.

HUGH KENNER, Professor Emeritus of English at the Johns Hopkins University, he is the leading critic of the High Modernists (Pound, Eliot, Joyce) and of Beckett. His books include *The Pound Era* and *The Stoic Comedians*.

GRAHAM HOUGH, Professor Emeritus of English at Cambridge University, is the author of, among other works, *The Dark Sun: A Study of D. H. Lawrence, The Last Romantics, A Preface to the Faerie Queene*, and *The Mystery Religion of W. B. Yeats*.

RICHARD ELLMANN, perhaps the leading literary biographer of our time, is Professor of English at Emory University, and formerly Goldsmiths Professor at Oxford. His major works include biographies of Yeats and Joyce, and a forthcoming life of Oscar Wilde.

BERNARD F. DICK, who teaches English at Fairleigh Dickinson University, has written several books on film as well as *The Hellenism of Mary Renault* and a study of William Golding.

ELEANOR COOK teaches at Victoria College, the University of Toronto. She is the coeditor, together with Chaviva Hosek, of *Centre and Labyrinth: Essays in Honour of Northrop Frye*.

GROVER SMITH, Professor of English at Duke University, has written on Archibald MacLeish as well as on T. S. Eliot.

GREGORY S. JAY teaches English at the University of Alabama. He has written extensively on contemporary criticism.

CLEO MCNELLY KEARNS teaches English at Rutgers University. She is the author of a forthcoming book on T. S. Eliot's poetry.

Bibliography

Ackroyd, Peter. *T. S. Eliot*. London: Hamish Hamilton, 1984.

Allan, Mowbray. *T. S. Eliot's Impersonal Theory of Poetry*. Lewisburg, Pa.: Bucknell University Press, 1974.

Bergonzi, Bernard. *T. S. Eliot*. New York: Macmillan, 1972.

Christ, Carol T. "T. S. Eliot and the Victorians." *Modern Philology* (November 1981): 157–65.

———. *Victorian and Modern Poetics*. Chicago: The University of Chicago Press, 1984.

Donker, Marjorie. "*The Waste Land* and the *Aeneid*." *PMLA* 89 (1974): 164–71.

Douglass, Paul. "The Gold Coin: Bergsonian Intuition and Modernist Aesthetics." *Thought* 58 (June 1983): 234–50.

Eliot, Valerie. *"The Waste Land": A Facsimile and Transcript*. New York: Harcourt Brace Jovanovich, 1971.

Everett, Barbara. "Eliot's Marianne: *The Waste Land* and Its Poetry of Europe." *The Review of English Studies* 31, no. 121 (1980): 41–53.

Frye, Northrop. *T. S. Eliot*. New York: Grove, 1963.

Gallup, Donald. *T. S. Eliot: A Bibliography*. Rev. ed. New York: Harcourt Brace Jovanovich, 1969.

Gardner, Helen. *The Art of T. S. Eliot*. New York: Dutton, 1959.

Grant, Michael, ed. *T. S. Eliot: The Critical Heritage*. 2 vols. London: Routledge & Kegan Paul, 1982.

Gray, Piers. *T. S. Eliot's Intellectual and Poetic Development 1909–1922*. Atlantic Highlands, N.J.: Humanities Press, 1982.

Headings, Philip. *T. S. Eliot*. New York: Twayne Publishers, 1964.

Hough, Graham. *Reflections on a Literary Revolution*. Washington, D.C.: The Catholic University of America Press, 1960.

Jay, Gregory S. *T. S. Eliot and the Poetics of Literary History*. Baton Rouge: Louisiana State University Press, 1983.

Kenner, Hugh. *The Invisible Poet: T. S. Eliot*. New York: Harcourt Brace Jovanovich, 1969.

———, ed. *T. S. Eliot: A Collection of Critical Essays*. Englewood Cliffs, N.J.: Prentice-Hall, 1962.

Lucy, Sean. *T. S. Eliot and the Idea of Tradition*. New York: Routledge & Kegan Paul, 1960.

Martin, Graham, ed. *Eliot in Perspective: A Symposium*. New York: Humanities Press, 1970.

Nevo, Ruth. "*The Waste Land*: Ur-Text of Deconstruction." *New Literary History* 13 (Spring 1982): 95–102.

Pinkney, Tony. *Women in the Poetry of T. S. Eliot*. London: Macmillan, 1984.

Richards, I. A. *Poetries and Sciences*. New York: Norton, 1970.

Rother, James. "Modernism and the Nonsense Style." *Contemporary Literature* 15, no. 2 (1974): 187–202.

Serio, John N. "Landscape and Voice in T. S. Eliot's Poetry." *Centennial Review* 24, no. 1 (Winter 1982): 33–50.

Smith, Grover. *T. S. Eliot's Poetry and Plays: A Study in Sources and Meaning*. Chicago: The University of Chicago Press, 1974.

———. *The Waste Land*. London: Allen & Unwin, 1983.

Tobin, David Ned. *The Presence of the Past: T. S. Eliot's Victorian Inheritance*. Ann Arbor: UMI Research Press, 1983.

Wilson, Edmund. *Axel's Castle*. New York: Scribner's, 1931.

Acknowledgments

"The Death of Europe" (originally entitled "The Death of Europe: *The Waste Land*") by Hugh Kenner from *The Invisible Poet: T. S. Eliot* by Hugh Kenner, © 1959 by Hugh Kenner. Reprinted by permission.

"Imagism and Its Consequences" by Graham Hough from *Reflections on a Literary Revolution* by Graham Hough, © 1960 by Catholic University of America, Inc. Reprinted by permission of the Catholic University of America Press, Inc.

"The First *Waste Land*" by Richard Ellmann from *Eliot in His Time*, edited by A. Walton Litz, © 1971 by Richard Ellmann. Reprinted by permission of the author and Princeton University Press.

"*The Waste Land* and the *Descensus ad Inferos*" by Bernard F. Dick from *Canadian Review of Literature* 2, no. 1 (Winter 1975), © 1975 by the Canadian Comparative Literature Association. Reprinted by permission.

"T. S. Eliot and the Carthaginian Peace" by Eleanor Cook from *ELH* 46, no. 2 (Summer 1979), © 1979 by The Johns Hopkins University Press. Reprinted by permission of the publisher.

"The Structure and Mythical Method of *The Waste Land*" (originally entitled "*The Waste Land* in the Making") by Grover Smith from *The Waste Land* by Grover Smith, © 1983 by Grover Smith. Reprinted by permission of Allen & Unwin.

"Discovering the Corpus" by Gregory S. Jay from *T. S. Eliot and the Poetics of Literary History* by Gregory S. Jay, © 1983 by Louisiana State University Press. Reprinted by permission.

"Eliot, Russell, and Whitman: Realism, Politics, and Literary Persona in *The Waste Land*" by Cleo McNelly Kearns, © 1986 by Cleo McNelly Kearns. Published for the first time in this volume. Printed by permission.

Index